PRAISE

*Sit, Cinder*

"Out of work in her forties, Lisa Cheek accepted a job offer that took her to China. Familiar work, but made seemingly impossible because Cheek spoke no Chinese. Nevertheless, she set out on what became an adventure into herself. It is a great story, a triumphant story well told, with the added bonus of two darling dogs that help along the way."

—**Abigail Thomas**, *New York Times* best-selling author of
*A Three Dog Life: A Memoir*

"Cheek takes us on a delightful and charming journey through an almost hidden part of the world. *Sit, Cinderella, Sit* has a bit of everything that you will want to read again and again."

—**Christy Warren**, author of *Flash Point*

"Here is a fresh voice, a wise old soul with a bouncy young attitude and the golden gift of capturing the bright shards of life. . . an unimaginable adventure filled with all the pain and joy of a complete life . . ."

—**Christopher Vogler**, author of *The Writer's Journey:*
*Mythic Structure for Writers*

"What an adventure! Lisa Cheek gives us a raw and heartfelt story any dog lover will relate to. Travel, dogs, and a peek into the unglamorous side of Hollywood by way of China—what more could a reader want?"

—**Teresa J. Rhyne**, *New York Times* best-selling author of
*The Dog Lived (and So Will I)* and *Poppy in the Wild*

"*Sit, Cinderella, Sit* is vivid, enticing, and heartfelt. I was right there with her minute by (often) uncomfortable and (very often) poignant minute."

—**Patti Eddington, author of** *The Girl with Three Birthdays*

"Lisa Cheek's can't-put-it-down memoir seems so blithely written, it feels like you're dishing about life with your best friend. All of a sudden, you realize you're smitten with the story and have been touched by its sweetness. Transfixed and transformed, I found magic on every page of this thoroughly delightful modern-day fairy tale."

—**Debra Landwehr Engle, author of** *The Only Little Prayer You Need*

"Refreshingly candid and insightful, *Sit, Cinderella, Sit* is an entertaining memoir of one woman's international journey in search of authentic love—for herself, for humanity, and for those powerful teachers we call dogs."

—**Michael Konik, author of** *Ella in Europe: An American Dog's International Adventure*

"With tenderness, wit, and curiosity, Lisa Cheek takes you on an eye-popping adventure that proves it's never too late to find your true place in the world."

—**Rona Maynard, author of** *Starter Dog: My Path to Joy, Belonging and Loving This World*

# SIT,
## CINDERELLA,
## SIT

# SIT, CINDERELLA, SIT

*A Mostly True Memoir*

# LISA CHEEK

SHE WRITES PRESS

Published 2025
Printed in the United States of America
Print ISBN: 978-1-64742-728-3
E-ISBN: 978-1-64742-729-0
Library of Congress Control Number: 2024915571

For information, address:
She Writes Press
1569 Solano Ave #546
Berkeley, CA 94707

*Interior design by Stacey Aaronson*

She Writes Press is a division of SparkPoint Studio, LLC.

Names and identifying characteristics have been changed to protect the privacy of certain individuals.

*For woman's best friend*

*"Life itself is the most wonderful fairy tale."*
—HANS CHRISTIAN ANDERSEN

*Once upon a time . . .*

*in the land of bright lights and glitz and glamour . . .*

*No!*

*Wait!*

*This isn't a fairy tale!*

*It's my life.*

# 1

IT WAS A DAY JUST LIKE ANY OTHER.

Bright morning sunshine streamed through the shutters in my treetop bedroom, bringing the start of another stunning Southern California day. Out from under the sheets popped a strawberry blond with white whiskers and fluffy pricked ears. Long, thin wisps of champagne-colored hair infused with a strand of licorice dangled from the tips of his ears, catching the sparkling sunlight. *This must be how angels look—a rescued one, without a care in the world.*

He gave a big yawn as he stretched his two front legs while staring at me with his soulful, big brown eyes.

"Good morning, Ron Howard. I take it you slept well. No bad dreams."

He had thick Pomeranian hair on a cairn terrier body, with a face that reminded me, and everyone he met, of their favorite teddy bear. He extended his neck toward the headboard, performing his morning stretch routine, his legs reaching toward the ceiling, looking like Winnie-the-Pooh—minus the too-small red T-shirt and pot of honey stuck on his head.

"I slept quite well. Thank you for asking," I informed him.

Ron Howard was my best friend and we'd had this morning ritual for five years now. A furry guru, he modeled for me the importance of warming up before facing the uncertainty of the day. As he moved, I moved—mirroring his routine.

During our first year together, Ron had his own bed on the floor. Being single, I felt it was important to keep the other side available for the man of my dreams. But a year came and went and no man appeared, so I invited my little guy into my bed and he'd been there ever since.

"A few more minutes and we gotta get our walk on."

He nuzzled his black button nose into my shoulder. Smart and intuitive, he understood I needed a few extra minutes to ponder what our day would be like. Mornings were my golden hour. Not only did I get to dream about what the day might bring us, I got to spend all of it with him.

Since he came to live with me, my life had changed considerably. People actually spoke to me. They wanted to meet Ron, stopping us on the street, sometimes driving by in a car, enthusiastically inquiring, "What kind of dog?" Some even stopped to take pictures, asking where I got him.

"He's a pound dog. A seventeen-pound dog," I'd tell them. Then they wanted to know which pound he came from. All ending our conversation with, "He's just so beautiful."

Before Ron, I would have passed by the strangers and said nothing. Now they wanted to meet him. It was like traveling with a celebrity. It was quite the honor being escorted everywhere by such a head-turner. The exchanges I had, however brief, had not only improved my social skills but, in a weird way, made me feel seen in the world. (Granted, no one asked about *me*—only Ron—but it taught me that everything wasn't always about me.)

I slipped my feet into woolly slippers and headed to the

bathroom, where I washed my face and lathered on SPF 40 sunscreen. Ron stumbled over a couple of pillows before he jumped off the bed while I walked into my mini walk-in closet and reached for my favorite Cath Kidston dress. I liked the way it made me feel—pretty and feminine. The way it skimmed my torso and flared out, it was the perfect everyday dress, falling just below the knees, giving the illusion I was ten pounds thinner.

I chose the navy-blue suede ballet slippers because they looked chic—the ideal shoe for walking around the neighborhood.

Ron patiently waited downstairs next to my tall shabby-chic Buddha statue until I arrived, and then, with a bounce in his step, led the way out the door.

This was *his* neighborhood. The only things that could break his stride were the German shepherds that lived on our block. Double his size, they'd bring out the worst in him, causing him to bark, yelp, and strain at his collar. This was the only time Ron ever lost his cool, but this morning there had been no sightings.

Jacaranda trees lined the street.

Soft purple blossoms carpeted the sidewalks and front lawns.

In the distance, I spotted Mavis, texting while walking. Sugar Ray, her eight-pound Maltese, followed. Sugar Ray was a senior dog when Mavis adopted him—ten, I think. She said he was a purebred, that he came with papers, but I never saw them. His original name was just Sugar, but Mavis added Ray to butch him up a little. Sugar Ray reminded me of Pig-Pen with his own cloud of dust that followed everywhere he went.

"Happy Friday!" Mavis shouted in her Kathleen Turner voice.

Mavis knew everything about everyone in our four-block radius. I nicknamed her The Mayor of 17th Street.

"So what are you up to today?" Mavis asked.

"It's been slow at the office. I'm hoping for a half day, to start the weekend early. You?"

Mavis's phone dinged. She looked down and frowned. "I've just picked up an assignment for the *LA Times*," she announced, never looking up, texting with the dexterity of a teenager.

A young man in well-worn jeans two sizes too big for him and a Dodgers baseball cap squatted down next to Sugar Ray and petted him under his chin. He looked up at Mavis.

"John, these are my friends Lisa and Ron Howard. Where are you off to this morning?"

"To get bagels. Want one?"

"I'm good, thanks." Mavis continued texting a short manifesto.

"Nice to meet you," John said with a grin before he walked toward the Boulevard.

*Whoosh* went Mavis's phone before she looked up.

"He's cute. I've never seen him around the neighborhood before."

"Just don't let him know where you live," she whispered.

"Why? He seems like such a sweet guy."

"He is and I'm sure there's nothing to worry about, but . . . he just got out of prison."

"Prison?"

"Prison. Did five years upstate for burglary." She nodded, looking off toward the Boulevard. "Don't tell him where you live."

*I wonder if he's single.*

# 2

"BON APPÉTIT." I SERVED RON DUCK AND POTATO FROM A CAN before I sat down at the table next to his bowl, my own bowl of granola sprinkled with organic blueberries.

A few minutes later, I raced upstairs, brushed my teeth, sprayed on my favorite scent, Eternal Optimist, and ran back downstairs for the five-block walk to work with Ron.

At the corner of the Boulevard, while we waited for the light to change, a red Honda hatchback whizzed by—its windows down—blaring Michael Jackson's "Beat It" as it ran the yellow light. A young man in Converse high-tops juggled five coffees and a large bag overflowing with pastries and breakfast sandwiches.

"No," I said as Ron pulled me toward the scent of pastries. "NO." Ron was quite the foodie.

The light for the oncoming traffic turned green, but Ron kept tugging until Mr. High-Tops dropped out of view.

"He wanted that guy's breakfast and wasn't gonna take no for an answer," chuckled Shirley. Sitting lotus position in her usual table at my favorite coffee shop, my eighty-year-old neighbor had a bird's-eye view of my latest Ron encounter. "You poor starving baby." She handed him a bit of her bran muffin. He gobbled it up and then licked her fingers clean.

"May I leave him with you while I pick up my coffee?"

"Sure. You're such a good boy," she said, speaking to him in a squeaky, high-pitched baby voice.

Inside, I inhaled the smell of freshly ground coffee beans while the sound of the frother enveloped me. For me, coffee was a necessary luxury. It was how I spoiled myself. Between the anticipation, the event, and the enjoyment, it was life at its finest. Coffee was the most important ritual of the day. It was like prayer. It brought me back to life each morning. Got the juices flowing. Made me take a second, third, and fourth look at things. I felt like I could do anything after a really good cup of coffee. And it needed to be that—A REALLY GOOD cup of coffee. I wouldn't drink that watered-down, bitter-with-an-aftertaste, room-temperature dribble that some called a cup of joe.

"I'll have a tall, half-caf, almond milk, extra-hot latte, please," I said to a green-haired barista I didn't recognize.

"No need!" The squeak of the swinging kitchen doors announced Shane, light hair with that day-old sexy stubble and the flawless orthodontist-perfected smile, as he pushed his way through the hectic counter.

"Your usual is ready. I saw you two crossing the street and Ron looked hungry, so I put a little something in the bag next to your coffee for him, too."

"You just made his day."

I thanked Shirley and took Ron's leash. We walked a few more blocks south until we reached a long and narrow building. Decades ago, it had been a train depot. Railroad tracks still ran through the parking lot. I released Ron's harness. He ran through the door, across the entryway, and behind the mahogany desk in the reception area.

"Good morning, Ron Howard."

Up from behind the desk appeared Blue . . . with Ron cradled in his arms.

Six foot five with dirty-blond dreadlocks halfway down his chest, he whistled *The Andy Griffith Show*'s theme song. Ron's head tilted back as he sighed, Blue's dreadlocks grazing his tummy. When Blue finished the closing chorus, he looked over at me. His aquamarine eyes—normally sparkling and clear—were bleary and bloodshot.

"Morning, Lisa."

He took the seat behind the hefty desk, continuing to hold Ron in one arm while he pushed a button on the switchboard below.

The company I worked for, Jump Cuts, was an "offline editing house," as they called it in the business. The way it worked was the script was written by the ad agency and sold to their client. Then a director was brought on board. He brought his production crew, consisting of five hundred people, from casting director to production designer. The whole film was shot in a day to a week.

Once shooting was wrapped, the footage was delivered to me in the form of "dailies," where I selected the best takes and crafted the story. The director was already off making bank at his next commercial while I was the one left to deliver the finished spot to make the client happy.

There's a famous saying, "We'll fix it in post." It's the one editors never want to hear. It means that we have a problem that should have been solved in production. Sometimes elements needed to tell the story were missing. Sometimes scenes that should have been filmed were not. Often special effect shots were not executed well—if at all.

All this to say it was my job to make it all work and deliver no matter what I was given. The pressure was on. The last person standing, I was responsible for color correction, music selection—mixed with a voice-over—and then sending it to a distribution house to be seen on a television near you.

"This is Blue. How may I help you? Please hold while I transfer you." He punched a few buttons and looked back at me. "All clear."

"How was your gig last night?"

"We didn't go on until one, so I'm going to need to take a nap. I checked the schedule. All the other edit bays are booked with our biggest client, Toy Couture, so I scheduled your office for my lunch hour." He held up his index finger. "Good morning. Jump Cuts. Please hold." He turned back to me. "Ron and I are dognapping your office."

"Great! Just what I needed. Nappers."

The building was cold and dark, which for an editing house was a good thing. The chill allowed the editing equipment to stay cool and not overheat, and the lack of windows not only kept the place cool but allowed the edit rooms to remain dark for optimal viewing. The atrium was furnished with brown leather couches and chairs, plenty of space for our clients, ad agencies, and directors to set up a virtual office. A vast skylight filled the center of the atrium, allowing it to be the one bright spot in the building.

I entered my edit bay, tossed the empty coffee cup into the trash can, and checked my messages. No flashing lights—not a job on the horizon. I left the room and headed up the open staircase that led to the second story of the atrium where the dining room, play area, and management offices were housed.

Our kitchen connected to an expansive playroom—a haven where clients could hang when they were not clustered in a dark edit cave. It consisted of a pool table that had once belonged to AC/DC, an acrylic foosball table, pinball machines, and vintage vending machines serving soda pop, snacks, and candy. No quarters needed. Everything was free.

Adjacent to the play area, on the island in the center of the kitchen, a colorful basket overflowed with blueberry, chocolate, and bran muffins. A large white bowl glistened with organic mixed berries and stacked on a separate platter, bear claws, glazed donuts, and banana nut bread. Apples, pears, and oranges, all arranged to perfection in another basket, were available for a grab-and-go kind of breakfast.

*BAM!* A tennis ball reverberated with a loud thud on the wall downstairs.

"Go get it, boy," Gary shouted from below.

I leaned over the open railing that encased the second floor and spotted Ron trotting back to Gary with a tennis ball in his mouth, his head held high.

"Good boy," Gary praised him.

*BAM!*

Tall, tanned, with thick, curly black hair, Gary was the owner of Jump Cuts. After he surfed in the mornings, he arrived in his signature racing-red Ferrari, sporting a freshly pressed white button-down with a pair of shorts, wearing the latest "must-have" sneakers and sunglasses nobody could afford.

I sauntered back into the kitchen where Stella, our craft services person, was busy wiping down the De'Longhi espresso machine Gary had brought back from a monthlong cooking holiday in Florence where he'd honeymooned with his third wife.

Stella's job was to keep the kitchen clean and stocked with expensive food. Decadence: the ultimate enticement in advertising to keep the clients happy and coming back. Stella had recently moved to Los Angeles to pursue her dream of designing costumes for Katy Perry. How she thought this craft services job in a dark editing house was a stepping stone to getting her there, I'd never know, but she had definitely perfected the art of a great latte. She wore crazy aprons that she'd designed and made. That particular day she was sporting a frilly bib with bows and ribbons sewn in a pattern of ice cream sodas and banana splits. Rhinestones and sequins trimmed the edges, making her sparkle as she spun around the kitchen.

"When you have a moment, would you make my usual?"

"Sure!" She wiped her hands on her apron and asked, "Watcha working on today?"

"Nothing. You?"

"Crazy busy. Final approvals with Toy Couture, so lots of people coming in," she said as she packed the espresso grounds tight before twisting the basket into the machine, locking it in. "We're ordering from your favorite place for lunch today." She whipped out the almond milk, made a half turn, and shut the door with her foot. "Oh, look who's here!" She gushed as she knelt to rub both her hands all over Ron's face, giving his ears an extra pat. "You are such a cute boy." His tail wagged like a windshield wiper in a rainstorm.

Salespeople, heads of divisions, and other muckety-mucks from Toy Couture paraded up the staircase and perused the counter of breakfast delights, cutting muffins in quarters, leaving dirty stirrers, empty sweetener packs, and coffee rings everywhere.

Pigs. All of them.

I stood against the kitchen wall, appalled, watching the Toy-ettes make a mess. I was overwhelmed with the urge to escape. On my flee downstairs, I followed Priscilla, the most senior producer, who was sashaying down the steps in her high-heeled designer pumps with white bell-bottoms. A neon-green headband stretched her shoulder-length bleached blond hair away from her surgically lifted face. As her heels hit ground, she clickety-clacked left and I made a sharp right into my edit bay.

Behind the tinted glass door to my office, I was ecstatic to be away from the craziness, safe in my little oasis where no one could see me stretched out on my sofa, reading a memoir someone had left behind.

Edit bays were dark, cozy places, and Ron was only too happy to snuggle beside me. He rested his head on my stomach and looked up at me as if I were about to read him a bedtime story. I had finally landed in my sanctuary.

"Hey, Lisa!" Blue boisterously strode in. "Lucky me! I got some extra minutes on my midmorning break to catch some additional z's!" He threw a blanket on the old chaise lounge tucked into the corner of my office. "Oh, and Gary wants to see you this afternoon before you leave."

*Great. Just great.*

# 3

SIX MONTHS EARLIER, GARY AND I HAD GOTTEN IN A HUGE fight when I'd lost Toyota, my number one client. He wanted me to replace Toyota with Toy Couture.

My unwavering position: *No, hell no. Advertising to children is wrong. Sets them up to fail. Their tiny minds have yet to develop. I've been a child and I remember watching television on Saturday mornings and needing Toy Couture's latest Bittie Kitties to add to my collection. I wanted everything. Hell, I still do. I'm sure it's hard enough being a parent today without being bombarded by your child needing Hollywood Hair Barbie or Malibu Beach Barbie.*

Ron and I moved out into the atrium, sat on the stadium-size sofa, and flipped through the trade magazines. *Advertising Age*, the *Hollywood Reporter, Variety,* and *Adweek.* It was all names and photos of people I didn't know, about new jobs they had accepted, and advertising campaigns they had collaborated on. I picked up another magazine and glanced through—more happy people working in their high-paying, successful jobs.

Mark, our humorless but diligent office manager, filled the empty pen boxes and placed new notepads on end tables.

Next to the pen box sat a small canister of dog treats. I took a few, marked the floor with a small *X* made from duct tape, showed it to Ron by touching it with my foot, then instructed

Ron to go to his mark. He padded over, stood on the *X*, and waited until I pointed my index finger down toward the floor. He sat tall and waited for his next cue.

"Good boy," I told him, followed by a couple of treats.

Then I took my hand, palm down, and motioned it toward the floor. Ron followed and lay down. I made a circle with my index finger and he rolled over. Placing my index finger by my ear and wiggling it, I said, "Speak," and he barked. He even knew how to "touch product" if I placed a can of dog food beside him.

Ron was a "working dog" and, by that, I mean he made money in TV commercials. He paid the mortgage one month starring in a Pedigree commercial. He even had an agent—something I had been unable to obtain for myself. At a big event in Beverly Hills one night, I finally met the *one* agent in Hollywood who represented both commercial and feature editors. And when I told him who I was, he furrowed his brow while looking like he'd just smelled a rotten egg and said, "I hated the guy in your movie."

"*LA Weekly*'s review spoke about how cleverly edited the movie was," I told him, wondering what "hating the guy" had to do with me and my talents. "How often does a review ever talk about the editing?"

"Yeah," he said as he rubbed his three-day-old chin stubble. "I just can't get past the annoying guy."

All my clients wanted Ron in their commercials, so we would practice his numerous tricks whenever we were waiting for changes from the client on our spots or waiting to get a job. These days we got a lot of practice in. I'd only had small jobs since Toyota left. I needed to land another big client, another car or a pharmaceutical account, but none of that was on the horizon. With ad agencies showing no interest in me, Jump Cuts had no need for me.

*Maybe I have this all wrong. Maybe, just maybe, Gary landed that BMW job for me.*

*Or maybe he double-booked us? Maybe he got Ron a national commercial to star in that I would be editing!*

After a half hour of anxiety and fantastical storytelling about where my job was headed, Gary returned from lunch, opened his office door, and motioned me in. I'd be put out of my misery at last.

"Thanks for stopping by, Lisa." I sat on a sleek leather couch while he leaned back in his Herman Miller chair. "We didn't get the BMW job. It went to some up-and-comer over at Slice and Dice."

"Did they say why?"

He leaned forward. "Listen, you should be thrilled you lasted as long as you did. You lasted longer than most. And you're a woman. You know it's all about youth in advertising."

*Lasted longer than most.* He made me sound like a loaf of bread. I loved advertising. It was the best job I'd ever had. Until . . . it didn't love me back.

"Lisa, we knew this day was coming."

"Yeah, I know. I just didn't think it was gonna be today."

The rumble of laughter and camaraderie grew louder downstairs—sports talk, cars, and motorcycles. All the other editors had received their Toy Couture approvals.

I had always been the only woman among a roster of men wherever I worked—where few were ever kind to me except when I was making *them* money. I was the number one biller for this company six out of the last seven years. I'd helped this man pay for his Bertram yacht, his second wife's Malibu beach house, his son's Harvard Law School education, and his third wife's fourth and fifth rehab.

"We sure are gonna miss you, Ron," Gary said as he rubbed him behind his ears. "Come on. Let's play some ball." Gary ran out of the office with Ron at his heels, his cross trainers squeaking all the way.

*That squeaking! Like dragging nails across the chalkboard.*

The building was now almost deserted—all the other editors had gone home to their wives and children, ready to enjoy what one did with their family on the weekend. The family life I never had. Most of the women who worked in that building were still single, yet every man was married and had a family. I'd given my life to this job, and for what? To be let go. To be told I was too old.

Stella wiped off the countertops, counting down the hours to fulfill her fifty-hour-a-week paycheck.

"Want to take some muffins or fruit home?" She handed me a brown paper bag.

Of course I did. I didn't have a paycheck anymore.

I walked over to the vending machine, placed my bag under the tray, and pulled the lever for the Hot Tamales until I had emptied the slot. Then I moved over and unloaded every slot, filling my bag with candy. I was in Vegas and winning every hand.

I cleaned out the refrigerator, helped myself to two bottles of red wine, and then reinvestigated the muffins and fruit that Stella had so generously offered and dumped the entire plate into my bag, placing the empty plate into the sink because I wanted to leave Stella with a clean kitchen. It wasn't her fault. She didn't even know they had just let the old nag go. Opened the barn and sent her out to pasture.

I turned around, taking one last look at the place that had fed me for the past seven years. While Pac-Man devoured those never-ending glowing dots, *wakawakawakawaka*, and Elton John's pinball machine clanged bells, I saddled Ron up and passed reception, where Blue flirted with Stella.

"Have a great weekend," I said as I leveled out the heavy contents in my backpack for the walk home.

"You, too. Bye, Ron," Blue said.

"See you Monday," Stella shouted as the door slammed shut behind us.

IT'S A FURRY FAIRY TAIL

# 4

an old-folks home in the ad business. One is long in the tooth once she hits forty in Hollywood, and I was not only over forty, but I was also a woman cutting TV commercials. Like spotting an albino mountain gorilla riding a polar bear while eating a pineapple on a safari in the Serengeti—there just weren't that many of us.

Sitting in a dark room, cutting television commercials was where I had a chance to show my clients what I thought.

How I saw their story.

The way I thought their story should be told.

And the most exciting part of it all . . .

I had only thirty seconds to convey a message.

To get your attention.

To get *you* to notice *my* thirty seconds.

Standing at my dining room table, in a townhouse I'd bought six years prior, I turned the backpack upside down, making it rain candy. Feeling like the most successful trick-or-treater returning home with the best haul, I sat down and ran my fingers through the pile of loot. There was enough to stuff my feelings down for the whole weekend and then some.

The wine I scored wasn't just any old wine. It was Gelfand's Shit-Faced Red, or "SFR"—the boss's favorite and hard to come by. He kept it hidden in the back of the rack, where no one ever looked. I poured myself what some might call a heavy pour—all the way to the top—and looked at Ron, who sat at my feet, looking up at me.

"Well . . . Ron, it's just you and me now. To us."

I raised my glass.

"Fuck it!" I put my glass down, picked up the bottle of SFR, and poured the wine down my throat. "Now that's how you toast *to us.*"

He stared at me.

For a long time.

I made him dinner to go with my wine.

He waited at attention for the habitual *bon appétit* before he began to dine.

With a knife and one of the Toll House cookie dough rolls in hand, I walked into my small sunken living room, past my grandmother's antique mirror. It was French rococo, ornate, with a cluster of flowers adorning the top of the gold gilt frame. In its heyday, it must have been beautiful, but it had become chipped and was missing many of its blooms. I caught a glimpse of my own reflection as I threw a strand of hair over my head, tucking it behind my ear, and headed over to my white linen sofa to collapse, letting out the longest and loudest sigh . . . a sigh that could have been mistaken for a cry.

In between slugs of wine, I cut into the cookie dough and scarfed down what was the equivalent of five baked cookies while I glanced around my living room. The three-thousand-dollar flat-screen Sony television glared back with a blurry, almost confused reflection of me. The overstuffed, bright red-and-purple-striped armchair I'd had reupholstered a few years back had begun to fade from the strong California sun. The unread paperbacks looked unloved from the built-in bookcase above.

Ron, full from dinner, trotted into the living room and leaped up on the sofa. After a few rounds of pushing and shoving one of the cushions, making it acceptable for him to lie down on, he curled up next to me.

Editing was like a jigsaw puzzle, and I was on the hunt to find the perfect pieces, to create the most masterful story from the material that had been entrusted to me. It was my responsibility to provide movement for the eye to follow through each frame as it revealed the next exciting visual. To create something that made you giggle or cry or just get your attention in a lineup of nine advertisements during your favorite TV show. Sure, it was a story that always ended with how extraordinary the product was and how it could make you feel invincible, but that's how I liked it.

A solution to your problem.

A happy ending.

I mean really, who doesn't love a happy ending?

By now I was using my fingers to dig into the tube of plastic cookie dough. Scraping the bottom with my fingers. I licked my fingers one by one, wiping raw dough onto my chin, cheeks, and nose. Coating the entire wine bottle in cookie dough as I chased it.

Ron placed his chin on my chest and looked up at me. His big brown eyes reminded me of Margaret Keane's paintings of children in the sixties and seventies. Such soulful eyes with so much to say behind them. As if he'd lived many lifetimes, per-haps more than me.

I tilted the bottle but missed my mouth, pouring it on Ron's head.

His blond locks, now deep red.

In my younger years, I was always on the road. One month I'd be cutting pretty pictures for Urban Outfitters, living on the forty-second floor of the Mandarin Oriental overlooking the Golden Gate Bridge, and the next month I'd be cutting comedy for Staples in Manhattan, returning to LA to cut a car spot that had been shot on the Road to Hana.

I felt the sugar rush hit my body . . . I was flying.

San Francisco.

New York.

Montreal.

But advertisers wanted young twenty-year-olds editing their ads. Not someone weathered and wrinkly with love handles. I squeezed the muffin top around my middle, dropped the wine bottle onto the floor, and crashed.

# 5

RON JUMPED UP AND DOWN ON MY CHEST LIKE A TRAMPOLINE.

I tried to open my eyes, but the overhead lights blared like a searchlight.

*Not now.*

*I can't.*

*My head hurts.*

I closed my eyes tighter.

His front paws jumped again on my chest . . .

"Okay. Okay."

He jumped onto the hardwood floor and broke into a tap dance. His nails struck out a rhythm, like something I'd heard the Blue Man Group perform.

I reached for my head, to hold it—massage it—comfort it, but my hand landed on my face and began peeling off the strands of hair glued to my cheek with cookie batter.

We fumbled out to the front of the building. It was past midnight, quiet, not a person in sight. The streetlamp buzzed above us while I wove back and forth as Ron got his much-needed relief. We stumbled back in, bumping into our fence not once, but twice, before reaching the front door. There would be bruises in the morning.

# 6

AFTER A SHOWER, I SHIMMIED INTO A BRAND-NEW PAIR OF leopard-print pajamas that I'd been saving for something special. Unemployed with a hangover on a Saturday morning: didn't get any more special than that. A shower, cup of coffee, and some glam jams began to put a girl back together.

We scrambled back into bed and turned on the television, flipping through channels until I landed on *Godzilla*. His monstrous tail flattened tall buildings while he waved his tiny arms toward an approaching helicopter as a squawking Rodan flapped his giant pterodactyl wings, smashing superstructures, demolishing cars, and terrorizing people. I was mesmerized watching them destroy the city. In a weird way, it brought relief and somehow made me feel slightly better watching my anger and disappointment being worked out through these monsters. But when the government wanted to take back their city and it got all bureaucratic, I got bored and hit NEXT. And then I ordered a pizza.

*WWE. Nope.*

*Next.*

*QVC.*

*Next.*

*Cocoon.* Ron Howard's movie.

"Look, Ron, your namesake. The director who makes everyone feel good. Just like you."

I reached for another bag of hazelnut M&M's and popped a few in my mouth.

"Let's watch the old people feel young again."

# 7

THE DOORBELL RANG.

"Delivery!"

Ron jumped up on his hind legs, sniffing the pizza box while I handed the delivery guy a twenty.

"Keep the change." I smiled, inhaling the basil and Italian spices that took me back to a sweet little restaurant in Naples, drinking the house wine while the waiter told me all about making his own red wine in his tiny vineyard overlooking the Mediterranean Sea.

I grabbed the other bottle of SFR and headed back upstairs with Ron so close at my heels I thought he'd slipped into my slippers. I caressed the bottle while I admired the simple, bright red label, knowing how perfect it would be with my pizza.

Last night's bottle was for misery and self-pity. Tonight was a night to begin to feel good again. Since I'd grabbed only two bottles of wine and I was unemployed, I didn't have time to wallow. I couldn't afford it—so I put on *Field of Dreams*. Kevin Costner was dreamy and I needed to go somewhere far from LA. A cornfield in Iowa felt like the place to be.

"To us," I said as I picked up my fancy bottle of wine, having learned last night that a glass is so unnecessary. "May we have a field of dreams of our own one day, Ron."

8

I reached for it.

Robert Owen, a feature cinematographer who was trying to cross over into directing commercials, was on the other end. Years earlier, Robert had needed someone to cut his reel, and a mutual friend suggested me. As he began to build his reel with a couple of public service announcements and spec spots (a commercial or preview to get us the job), I was always his first call.

Robert knew everyone. Roy Oldman—the five-time Academy Award nominee for his cinematography—liked what I had cut for Robert, so Roy hired me to put together the American Society of Cinematography awards show one year. Not only was it the biggest honor, but it was every editor's dream to stare at the most beautiful images ever shot—all shown on one enchanting evening where I met Hollywood's most famous filmmakers.

Definitely a night to remember.

And Robert, like everyone else in Hollywood, had a personal project, a film he talked about every time I saw him that he was going to make one day, and at *two forty-five in the morning Pacific Coast Time*, he wanted to tell me his dream had come true. His dream of telling the original version of the Cinderella story . . .

after having discovered it was originally written in China around 768 AD. He'd secured his last funding and now had the money to hire me again.

"Hello."

"Have you packed your bags yet?"

"Huh?"

"Lisa?"

"Yes."

"Robert here."

"Robert, uh, hello."

"I need to know you're coming. I have the money for you to come. The producer is pounding out the finishing schedule as we speak."

*Wow. This is happening.*

I reached for the coffee cup and drank yesterday's day-old sludge.

"Robert, I'm flattered you want me to edit your film. I know how personal this story is to you, but I don't speak Mandarin. Fuck, I barely speak English."

As Ron watched me from the top of my pillow, staring intently, it seemed as if he knew I was talking about traveling.

"Don't be silly, Lisa! It's the Cinderella story. Everyone speaks Cinderella. The shoe, the ball gown, the fairy godmother, the carriage."

Cold pizza and a lone well-worn UGG boot stared back at me while Robert continued, "Besides, there's hardly any dialogue in the movie. You read the script."

I had read the script two years ago. I just never thought we would be here, in pre-production. I never ever thought this would really happen. Nobody ever finds funding for their scripts.

"It's the original telling of 'Cinderella.' People need to know it came from China. The mountains, the rice fields, the ancient temples. It's a part of the world no one has ever seen. We can show them. I know how technically challenged you are, and I've taken care of that. I got you the best assistant. He's an engineering genius and he speaks four languages. He'll set you up, load your files, keep a backup system for you. He will take great care of you. All you need to do is focus on the story and say yes."

I thought back to when I saw *Cinderella* for the first time. I was five. It was the most magical story. My favorite fairy tale.

"I want you here in six weeks. It will be the last week of pre-production, giving you time to get over jet lag, so you can hit the ground running."

"Wow . . . that's . . . soon. But, Robert . . ."

*Click*, and he was gone.

My head began to spin.

My heart began to race.

My life had just gotten turned upside down . . . again.

A job?

I'd just lost a job.

I just got a job.

A job reporting the first narrative of the Cinderella story was always just a dream. A fairy tale. It was never supposed to come true. Who went to the middle of China and cut a movie in Mandarin when they spoke only English?

*Robert!*

*Crazy!*

*Did I just have this conversation?*

*Maybe I was dreaming the dream.*

*A hungover dream? No more Shit-Faced Red for me!*

*Six weeks to be in China?*

*Really?*

*I'd have to leave Ron.*

*I have no one to take care of him.*

*We've never been apart for longer than two weeks!*

I inhaled.

I exhaled.

I inhaled.

I needed fresh, hot coffee.

I needed a fairy godmother . . . I had no idea what was real or make-believe . . . I looked over at Ron, who was looking up at me.

# 9

SUNDAY MORNINGS WERE ALWAYS THE QUIETEST DAY IN THE neighborhood.

Ron sat still at the corner, waiting to be told it was safe to cross the street. In my head, a large traffic jam appeared—information coming from all directions, horns blaring, demanding my attention. Robert hadn't given me time to give him an answer, and six weeks was *no* time to get ready. Ron would think he had been abandoned again if I left him, and I wouldn't know how to work without him. It had been five years since I adopted him, but it felt as if he'd been by my side for like . . . forever. I shook my head, trying to shake off the noise, and looked both ways. Not a car in sight.

"All right," I whispered.

It had been ten years since I cut a feature where I had my own little Cinderella story, editing a tiny film, *20 Dates*. The director and I wrote the whole movie in my edit bay. The print was still wet when we boarded the plane to Park City, Utah, for the Slamdance Film Festival. Twenty-four hours, one award, and a review in the *Hollywood Reporter* later, Fox Searchlight bought it. I spent the next six months working on the Fox lot. It was a filmmaker's dream: to see their name on the big screen at their local movie theater.

But a chance to go to a part of China I'd never seen, that most people had never heard of, now *that* sounded exciting.

Still, leaving Ron wasn't my only concern.

*What about my townhouse?*

*How would I pay my bills?*

Up ahead was a cloud of smoke. Mavis and Sugar Ray emerged through the haze. On weekends, Mavis could be found smoking instead of texting. She smoked like she texted—fast and with a purpose.

With another hot day ahead, Mavis had dressed for it in her bright red tank top, shorts, and flip-flops. Underneath her left bra strap, tucked in tight, perched a box of Marlboro Lights, her bright pink Bic lighter rattling inside the box.

Mavis and Sugar Ray shuffled their way along the sidewalk like aging rock stars.

"Hey, Ron Howard," Mavis called out while Sugar Ray stopped to take a poop on an immaculate manicured lawn. Every blade of grass was the same shade of green and the exact same height. Not a weed in sight. Mavis puffed on her morning cigarette and then snuffed it out on the sidewalk.

A stout woman sporting a striped terry cloth robe with her head filled with pink sponge curlers leaned out her front screen door, yelling, "My yard is not a toilet for your dog!"

Mavis exhaled her smoke toward the woman and then politely responded, "Lady, to a dog, the whole world is a toilet."

Unruffled, she leaned down, picked up his miniature poo with a plastic bag, tied it off in a knot, and stared me down.

"What happened to you?"

I filled Mavis in on my life, the last forty-eight hours of it.

"Why wasn't I invited to the wine and candy party? Hot

Tamales are my favorite and I believe you are what you eat," she said with a grin before she lit another cigarette.

"There's plenty left if you want to come over."

"Wow, China. That's fabulous!"

Ron sat at my feet, his sweet body leaning against my legs.

"How can I leave Ron that long?"

"Don't be silly. He can stay with us. There's always room for one more in my king-size bed." Mavis chuckled.

I looked down at Sugar Ray. Dust and tiny insects flew around his body the way planets circled the sun. He sat with his left hind leg over his head while he licked his butt. Then I looked over at Ron. He sat as if he were waiting for morning inspection. Back straight. Head held high. Eyes straight ahead. I wanted to pin a medal on his chest, he looked so regal.

"An old friend of mine from *The New Yorker* is coming out here to cover a story," Mavis said. "He needs somewhere to stay. Sounds like your place might be available?" Mavis waved her cigarette as if it were a wand. "What does a girl wear to edit a movie in China, anyway?"

# 10

BACK AT HOME, I HAD JUST SETTLED IN WHEN MY PHONE RANG.

"It's Eva, the line producer. I want to make sure you have received the letter of introduction I emailed you this morning so you can apply for your work visa ASAP."

"I did."

I reached for Ron, sitting next to me on the sofa, his head resting on a throw pillow, and began rubbing his ears while I cradled the receiver.

"We are dealing with a time crunch now, so first thing tomorrow, I need you to get the ball rolling."

An American expat, Eva had grown up in Santa Barbara and moved to Shanghai after college to work in the film business. There was an enthusiasm in her voice that made me like her right away. Women were few and far between in the business, and with her being bilingual, I was sure she was in great demand.

"So what do I need to know about where we're going?" I reached for a pen and pad of paper.

"Well, we'll be shooting in the Yunnan Province. It's in the southwestern part of China. I've never been, so I'm afraid I can't tell you much more—other than our schedule."

I scribbled "Yunnan."

"You'll fly into Kunming and then the shoot travels north along the Tibetan border."

Beneath "Yunnan," I wrote "Kunming."

"There will be daylong driving on windy dirt roads between locations. One—Stone City—is quite the journey to get to."

I added "Stone City."

"Robert told you it's an entirely Chinese crew, right?"

I studied the names of the places I had written down, hoping I spelled them correctly so I could look them up as soon as I was off the phone.

"And by Chinese, I mean they don't speak a word of English."

"Uh-huh." I wondered if it was Hunan or Szechuan food that was eaten in Yunnan and thought I'd google it later. I loved spicy food.

"Your assistant, Max, will be your translator."

I scribbled Max's name onto the notepad.

"I will have him call you this week so you can brief him on what you need. We need to take everything with us. We can't expect to find anything in these locations. Some of them take a donkey ride to get to."

*A donkey ride?*

"Get the visa going. Pay for the expedited process—we'll reimburse you. Things move a lot slower in China. I'll email your travel arrangements and a list of all our locations with the preliminary schedule. Oh, and Robert needs you to bring a Starbucks care package. I'll send his order. Coffee is not a thing here in China, so if you are a big coffee drinker, you might want to do the same for yourself."

I wrote down "Starbucks."

"I'll email you from now on, or we can Skype. Skype's big here. Email any questions. Okay?"

"Okay, thanks, Eva."

*No Starbucks? What was I getting myself into?*

The atlas was heavier than I remembered, although I couldn't remember the last time I'd looked at it.

Sitting cross-legged on the floor, I flipped through the pages until I found China. It was broken down into several sections. I searched for Yunnan. And then Kunming. I ran my finger across the paper. It was mountainous, all right. I could practically feel the inclines.

Ron placed his paw on the map, gazed up at me, and stared deep into my eyes without blinking, then rolled onto his back and reached for the ceiling with his paws. It was his way of asking for a belly rub.

# 11

IT WAS ONE OF THOSE TALL GLASS BUILDINGS ON WILSHIRE BOULEVARD in Westwood.

I walked up to the information desk and stood behind a man dressed in military fatigues with a gray parrot on his shoulder. Helping him was a young man named Carlos, according to the name embroidered on his shirt pocket.

"You can't handle the truth," squawked the parrot as he paced back and forth on his right shoulder.

"General Patton is my therapy bird," the man in fatigues explained.

"I understand, sir." Carlos picked up the phone at his desk.

"I can't go anywhere without him." General Patton marched up his right shoulder, about-faced, and shrieked, "We live in a world that has walls."

"Let me get my supervisor." Carlos punched in some numbers.

"Your tone of voice is upsetting the general," he said to Carlos, who backed away from the counter, eyes locked on the bird.

"We follow orders, son. We follow orders or people die," General Patton squawked.

As entertaining as this was, I needed my visa, and it didn't help that Carlos was preoccupied.

I needed to find my way to China. I scanned the building directory by the elevators: EXPEDITE SERVICES, SUITE 426.

There were three tall elevator doors with several people gathered in front of each one, all watching the floor numbers as they lit up. Two impatient men in suits checked their phones, one letting out a loud sigh every time the elevator moved up instead of down, the other man texting as if it were his last text. So much to say, so little time to say it.

They shuffled back and forth in front of the three different elevator doors like pawns in a chess game.

A bell rang. Doors opened.

A few of those waiting smiled as if they had hit the jackpot, and others started to enter—elbowing and pushing their way into the mob of people spilling out into the lobby.

The doors closed as quickly as they opened.

I waited for the next one to arrive and hopped on, pressing the number four. Standing in front of the floor numbers, I hit each button as the passengers shouted their lucky numbers. "Twenty-first floor!" "Twenty-eight, please!" "Nine!"

The doors closed and we were on our way only to stop on the next floor up, level two.

Level two was parking, so no one got off. More people got on, pushing me toward the back. The doors closed again and up we went, stopping on the third floor, loading more passengers from the carpark. Now we were packed like Styrofoam peanuts in a box of bone china teacups as the door closed.

The doors flew open. No one moved.

"This is my floor!" I shouted from the back of the elevator.

One person stepped off while the others played Twister, bending their bodies, torquing into awkward poses, making sure that under no circumstances a foot leave the elevator floor. I pushed my way through, landing on the other side of the doors as they began to close.

The fluorescent lights above flickered in a non-rhythmic pattern while a constant high-pitched hum buzzed as I walked down the long, narrow hallway.

Beside the office door, in black removable lettering: SUITE 426. The top of the 6 had dropped down, making it look like a 9. Propping open the door was a dented, commercial-size can of black-eyed peas and the overwhelming smell of bananas. A banner hung on the wall—EXPEDITED SERVICES DELIVERED IN A FLASH. I walked to the desk and tapped the bell. A man in desperate need of a haircut and shave appeared from the back room. He looked as if he could use a good night's sleep.

"I'm Moe," he said, wiping his sweaty palm on his wrinkled khakis before extending his right hand.

"I need a visa for China ASAP."

He looked like an unmade bed—shirt with a stain the shape of Texas, sweat oozing from his forehead, black-rim Ray-Bans askew on his nose.

We shook hands, then I wiped my palm on my trousers.

"I have to leave in six weeks, so I'll be needing a rush on this."

Moe looked down at his shirt and handed me a clipboard, a packet of forms, and a pen.

"I'll need you to answer all the questions." Then he disappeared.

I sat down in the dreary waiting area to fill out the papers and rang the bell again.

Moe reappeared with a price list:

*$500 for the visa*

*$50 postage from LA to the consulate in New York*

*$50 postage from New York to LA*

*$150 for expedited service including photographs*

"Seven hundred and fifty dollars?" I asked.

"Seven fifty and your visa will be good for six months." Moe nodded while saying yes.

"Six months?"

"Yes, six months. I need you to step into this room for a photograph."

I followed him into what felt like an interrogation room, tiny and windowless. I stepped over an overflowing trash can. A black banana peel thrown over the top, looking like a dead octopus in a sea of trash, stared back at me.

*This is beginning to feel like a scene from a horror movie.*

*Or a Lifetime movie where the lead is running away from her old life only to be murdered by a serial killer. Women are always being murdered in Lifetime movies. So why, why, why is it called a channel for women?*

Moe ran behind the camera twisting knobs, adjusting the height.

"Ready?"

I forced a grin.

"No, no. No smiling," Moe shouted from behind the camera. If this were a Lifetime movie, this was the moment he would kill me.

Moe snapped a photo and ran to answer the phone, knocking over a pile of papers. "Expedite Services."

A tall man in a pin-striped suit entered and rang the bell just as Moe was finishing the call. "Yes! Yes! We are open till five. Walk-ins welcome. No appointment needed."

He hung up the phone.

"You here for a visa?" he asked the tall man.

"Yes, I'm traveling to Azerbaijan."

Out came the clipboard, forms, and pen.

He called to me: "No good. You closed your eyes. We need to do it again."

I stared into the lens like the woman in *American Gothic*, stoic and stern.

"Good one."

I handed Moe my credit card. "I will get the visa before I leave?"

The phone rang.

Moe answered, "Expedite Services. Please hold."

He covered the receiver with his hand. "Good for six months."

# 12

INSIDE MY BRAND-NEW SUITCASES WITH THE FANCY SPINNER wheels lived a vast emptiness that would hold my necessities for the next three months. Except for Ron.

*Focus, Lisa. You'll be back.*

The mantra made the idea of traveling without him bearable.

One suitcase for clothes.

The other for work and supplies.

I'd been an Avid editor for almost twenty years, but I had decided to go with Final Cut, a new software at the time, because the system was so much cheaper. I hired a tutor, watched every video on YouTube, and was assured that Max knew Final Cut inside and out. I packed my *Final Cut for Dummies*, a well-worn gel wrist-rest for the keyboard, trusty trackball, and two thumb drives loaded with my user settings.

Ron didn't move as he watched me from atop the bed, his big brown eyes boring a hole in my heart.

Since Eva said they didn't serve milk in China, I resolved to live without it. Go local and drink tea. I packed Robert's Starbucks haul next to several boxes of PowerBars for our road trips.

"I think twenty pairs of underwear is enough, don't you?" I asked Ron, even though I wasn't sure I had a right to engage him in this activity since I was leaving him behind.

But Ron was bigger than that. He lifted his head off the pillow as if to nod.

"Makes it easier to find them this way."

Having spent much of my life traveling, I'd picked up a few good hacks. One was to pack similar items in plastic bags. The second was to pack the oldest stuff I owned. I threw in two pairs of pajamas—one flannel, the other cotton, so I was prepared for any kind of weather. Two pairs of cashmere socks, a lavender cashmere wrap, and one that could double for a blanket.

I packed seven long-sleeve black T-shirts and five pairs of black sweatpants, zippering them into their own bag and placing them on top of the T-shirts. In the closet, I reached for one black cotton and one black cashmere pullover sweater, tossed them in a bag together, and pulled out my down zip-up jacket.

Done.

Everything matched.

*Shoes! I almost forgot shoes.*

I looked down at the floor in the closet.

Rows and rows of pretty shoes.

I reached toward the back for a pair of well-worn New Balance tennis shoes and a pair of black Mephisto walking shoes.

These would take me to places I'd never been before.

# 13

TWO OVERWEIGHT BAGS SAT BY THE FRONT DOOR, BELTED, tagged, and ready, the taxi ordered.

Mavis wanted me to leave Ron with her the night before, but I needed one more night with my little guy.

I turned out the bedside light, scooted under the covers, and stared over at Ron. He yawned, his tiny, jagged teeth on display. All four legs stretched away from his torso while he let out a large and long sigh through his nose. Today had been a long day and it was way past our bedtime.

"I guess you know by now I'm leaving. I gotta go away for three months and I can't take you with me."

I took a deep breath and held it in, hoping that would make time stop and I could have this moment forever with Ron, without crying. But I couldn't. Within minutes, I was a snotty, wet mess.

"Mavis and Sugar Ray are gonna take great care of you while I'm gone."

I stroked the hair between his ears. Long, thin wisps fell off the tips, dancing in the streams of light the way I imagined fairies did every day, in the sunshine on dewdrops in a garden, filled with dandelions waiting to be picked so they could make wishes like never having to leave their best friend behind come true.

# 14

MY PHONE DINGED.

I looked at the clock. 6:55 a.m.

*Shit! I forgot to set the alarm!*

I threw back the covers and checked my phone.

*Cab's here.*

I jumped into the clothes I'd laid out the night before, brushed my teeth, and snatched one of the pillows Ron liked to sleep on, plus a T-shirt from the dirty clothes basket, and carried them downstairs. One of Ron's tennis balls lay beside Buddha. I slipped it into his pillowcase.

With my arms overflowing, I informed the cab driver, "We have one quick stop before the airport."

Nestled in the back of the cab, I held Ron close and whispered in his ear, "I'm coming back for you."

It started sprinkling. And in LA, that could shut down the whole city, causing me to miss my flight. I grabbed his pillow and my T-shirt and slipped out of the taxi with Ron on my hip, navigating the drizzle to Mavis's apartment.

"Good morning, guys. We're ready for walkies," she said, taking Ron's leash.

"Here's my T-shirt. You might want to have it around him for the first few days, just 'cause it smells like me." I stuck my hand down the side of the pillowcase for Ron's tennis ball and slipped it into my coat pocket before handing the pillow over to Mavis.

She handed me a small, wrapped package. "Open this in the cab," she said.

"Thank you."

I leaned down and gave Ron a kiss on the head. "I'll be back for you," I told him, again, wishing he understood.

"Now go before you miss your plane." Mavis shooed me toward the door. "He'll be fine. Great. And *yes*, I'll stay away from the German shepherds."

"Thank you again, Mavis. I'll Skype first chance I get."

"Go give Cinderella the happy ending she deserves," Mavis said as I hugged her goodbye and got into the cab, stifling tears.

"Bradley Terminal, please." I tucked the package from Mavis into my carry-on and turned around to watch Ron from the rear window. He stood stiff like a statue as he watched us drive away down the street all the way to the corner, where we turned right on Wilshire Boulevard, until I couldn't see him anymore.

# 15

WHILE THE TSA AGENT STUDIED MY PASSPORT PHOTO, I studied her bouffant hairdo. It was a work of art, teased and sprayed so high it made her a full three inches taller. I ran my fingers through my own hair, fluffing it up at the roots.

"Honey, you all right? Your eyes are all puffy and your face is swollen like you been stung by a colony of bees."

She wasn't wrong. After leaving Ron standing on the sidewalk, I could only imagine what I must look like, having cried all the way to the airport.

"I heard there is a great new cover-up at the Dior counter in Duty-Free. You might want to have a look after you get through with security."

I put on my sunglasses and meandered my way through the roped-off lines until I caught up with a man and his little daughter, about five years old. He held her small hand in his. In her other hand was a much-loved teddy bear. Most of his fur was gone. His neck was held together in large, dark brown stitches, as if he had been hugged so much he'd been decapitated once or twice.

"I had one of those. His name was Theodore," I told her.

She looked up at me and then grinned at her father. I

smiled and thought about where I was headed . . . and the last time I'd cut a feature with Robert, more than a decade ago. Back then, he and his wife had just adopted their Chinese daughter, Nia. A toddler, she'd waddled barefoot into the edit bay every day, carrying a half-eaten hot dog.

I made my way through security and to my gate.

"Flight 946 to Hong Kong is boarding all rows."

I walked to the back of the plane and an aisle seat, which was the only way I traveled given my claustrophobia. Any seat under the overhead compartment made me feel closed in and caused me to hyperventilate. I'd been known to take off my clothes, pant like a dog, and scream, all at the same time.

The doctor had loaded me up with all the pills I needed. Lorazepam for nerves, Ambien for jet lag, acetazolamide for altitude sickness, and Tamiflu in case of bird flu. He'd made sure I'd been inoculated for hepatitis A, hepatitis B, yellow fever, tetanus, and the flu. I was a traveling pharmacy.

Opening the storage compartment above my head, I moved a nylon backpack to make room for my coat and carry-on. As I shoved my bag to the back, Mavis's package fell out into the aisle. I'd totally forgotten about it. On top, there was a handwritten note in black pen: "May these help you cut your feature faster and bring you back home safely."

I tore into the wrapping. Inside was a pair of hot pink, fingerless, cashmere gloves. I slipped one on each hand and pulled them all the way up to my elbow. I felt like old Hollywood in them, a punk version of Audrey Hepburn.

"Flight attendants, please take your seats."

As our plane idled on the runway waiting for takeoff, I thought about how Robert had discovered the world's earliest version of "Cinderella" and wanted to make it into a movie, leaving it as a gift to Nia.

The engines roared and my armrests shook as we gathered speed down the airstrip.

I closed my eyes and took in two slow, deep breaths.

No turning back now.

# 16

IT WAS BRAVE FOR ROBERT TO WRITE AND DIRECT A MOVIE in China, especially since he'd never written or directed anything before this, other than a few commercial spec spots and public service announcements. And now, he was counting on me to edit his first feature film . . . in China.

After a fifteen-hour flight, I had nine hours to contemplate the magnitude of that fact before my next one to Kunming.

Hong Kong's airport felt like Rodeo Drive on a blindingly bright day. I put on my sunglasses and wandered the terminal, watching people run to their gates or wander in a daze, having just deplaned.

Jet lag wasn't the only thing in the air. The smell of garlic, ginger, and soy sauce infused with the searing sound of hot oil popping in woks surrounded me as I walked through a string of small restaurants.

An easel stood outside the entrance to Happy Ho's with pictures of dishes that looked fresh and healthy. With my eyes closed, I took in the intoxicating fumes and decided to grab a seat at one of the two empty tables. A scrawny young Asian man dressed in all black stood directly behind me, speaking perfect English. "Today's special is fried rice with one meat and tea, thirty dollars."

"I'll take it."

"Chicken, beef, pork, or shrimp?"

"Shrimp, please."

"Jasmine or green tea?"

"Jasmine."

After lunch, I wandered farther into the terminal toward Bulgari, Chanel, Cartier, and Dior.

Jet-setters dressed in designer rags strutted from boutique to boutique, staring at the latest collections, a luxury bag hung from every arm.

I moseyed through the handbags.

Caressed the leather.

Admired the hardware.

Then strolled through the scarves.

Drooled over the color palettes and designs.

I roamed in and out of the jewelry stores, ogled watches, eyed diamonds, coveted pearls.

In the distance, I spotted the IMAX movie theater. A red carpet led up to the box office where a young girl with a high ponytail and a mole under her lower lip sat behind the kiosk.

"What's the next show?" I asked.

"The matinee is *Bolt*." She smiled, flashing a mouth filled with braces covered in neon green and orange rubber bands.

"The movie about a dog?"

She flashed another smile as she pointed to the movie poster behind her. "Yes. *Bolt*, the animated children's movie."

"One ticket, please." I fumbled through my backpack for my credit card.

"Where would you like to sit?"

"Last row. Aisle seat, please."

The spacious lobby was dressed in shades of blue. Thick, plush, aqua-blue wall-to-wall carpet covered the floor. Elegant, marine-blue velvet curtains swayed from the ceiling, puddling on the carpet below. I expected Ariel or Nemo to swim up, collect my ticket, and take me to my seat. Instead, I handed my ticket to an old gentleman with a super-long pinky fingernail, who tore the ticket in half.

Small children of every nationality ran shrieking around droopy-eyed parents, who leaned against the wall of the lobby, fenced in by their carry-ons. Tiny sweaters and scarves, stuffed animals, and sippy cups hung from their limbs; exhaustion seeped from their pores. Tiny voices squealing in every language rang out. An international *Romper Room*.

*And that is why I don't have children.*

I walked to the candy counter.

"One Grand Palace, please," I ordered, which consisted of popcorn and a drink.

"Would you like lychee, sweet and sour, strawberry, or butter flavor on your popcorn?"

"Butter, please."

"Choice of drink?"

"Cherry Coke, please."

"Three hundred fifty dollars."

*Three hundred fifity dollars? That's like forty-seven US dollars. I could dine at a fancy restaurant on Rodeo Drive while enjoying a medium-well petite filet mignon with glass of champagne for that!*

Everything was expensive. And there was so much to do. There was an aviation museum, a spa, a golfing area, and an art museum. I thought there was even an amusement park with a carousel and a Ferris wheel, though I didn't have time to check it out. If I didn't know better, I'd have thought this *was* Hong Kong.

I entered the massive theater and settled in, using my winter coat as a blanket, wishing Ron were here to watch the movie with me.

# 17

UPON ARRIVAL AT THE KUNMING AIRPORT, WE EXITED THROUGH the outside staircase, allowing me to move my body in the sunlight for the first time in over two days. It felt good to breathe in something that wasn't day-old body odor or toilets that needed cleaning, even if it was jet fumes from planes idling.

We crossed the tarmac, dodging baggage handlers and mechanics as we approached the terminal.

After collecting my checked bags, I turned toward immigration.

Behind the glass window sat a bald gentleman with a crooked nose.

I placed my passport and letter of introduction through the slot between us.

He gave me a good long stare that included a squint before he flipped through the first few pages of my passport.

Then he returned to my photograph.

Studied it.

Then studied me.

Then studied it.

Then studied me.

He squinted again—tilting his head to the left and then to the right.

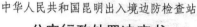

中华人民共和国昆明出入境边防检查站

# 公安行政处罚决定书

昆公境（检）决字 [2009] 第 030001 号

　　被处罚人 CHEEK LISA COLLEEN，女，1962 年 03 月 29 日生，美国人，持 208752600 号美国普通护照，现住美国。

　　现查明当事人于 2009 年 2 月 9 日持第 208752600 号美国护照和第 C9580010 号中国访问（F）签证从昆明口岸入境后，超过签证允许的停留期限，在华逾期居留四十一（41）日（该签证为中国驻洛杉矶使领馆于 2009 年 1 月 22 日签发，签证有效期至 2009 年 7 月 22 日，一次入境后可在华停留 30 日）。当事人的行为已构成在华非法居留的违法事实。

　　以上事实有当事人所持的护照资料页、签证复印件、入境记录、出境卡、登机牌复印件等证据证实。

　　根据《中华人民共和国外国人入境出境管理法实施细则》第四十二条第一款，现决定给予被处罚人罚款人民币伍仟元整的处罚。

　　履行方式：因被处罚人在当地无固定住所，不当场收缴事后难以执行，根据《公安机关办理行政案件程序规定》第一百六十六条第一款第（四）项之规定，决定当场收缴罚款。

　　被处罚人如不服本决定，可以在收到本决定书之日起六十日内向云南省公安边防总队申请行政复议或在三个月内依法向昆明市官渡区人民法院提起行政诉讼。

　　附：／共／份

二〇〇九年四月二十二日

被处罚人（签名）　*Lisa Cheek*
2009 年 4 月 22 日

交被处罚人

"You here for work?"

"Yes." I gave him the largest grin I could muster.

"What kind of work?"

Now, I knew it was never a good idea to say you were a jour-nalist or in the entertainment business, as many governments did not want people reporting on their country, and I'd also seen the infamous *Midnight Express* prison scene, but I had already been granted my work visa, so I pointed to the letter of introduction.

"I'm here to edit the original 'Cinderella' story."

He examined the letter again, studying each character on the page. Then he stuffed the letter back into my passport, stamped a page with an ink chop, handed it back to me, and waved me through.

Men in mismatched suits, wearing black dress socks and slip-on plastic sandals, smoked cigarettes as they held signs. I scanned them, looking for someone who would be looking for someone like me.

"Lisa! Lisa!" A young Asian man, completely the antithesis of all the drivers, sporting wire-frame glasses, jeans, and a navy down jacket, stepped toward me with purpose.

"I'm Max," he said with a warm, open smile as he shook my hand with excitement.

"So good to finally meet you."

"Here, let me help you."

He transferred my backpack from my arm to his back.

"This is Vin—our driver."

Vin stood tall and lanky, a cigarette hanging from his lips. I leaned in to shake his hand, but he reached for the handle of my suitcase trolley instead. Max said something to him in Mandarin and he nodded. I put my hands in my pockets and found Ron's tennis ball. I held it, squeezed it, wishing he were by my side on this new adventure.

A second wind kicked in with the excitement of meeting Max and Vin.

Vin stopped to put out his cigarette, only to light another one. *A chain-smoker.*

It was a good five-minute trek through the parking lot as we navigated a sea of cars until we arrived at a white van. Vin opened the back doors and began rearranging the back seat, knocking cigarette ashes all over the interior.

I sat up front, while Max explained it was a full day's drive with a stop for lunch. He reminded me to wear my seat belt, then jumped in the back seat.

"Your English is perfect. I hear you speak other languages," I said to Max, pulling the windshield visor down to get relief from the bright sun. The mirror on my visor allowed me to make eye contact with him, so I didn't have to turn around.

"I speak Mandarin, Cantonese, Taiwanese, and English. I can get by in several other languages but not like I do with these four." He fastened his seat belt.

"Wow. I can barely speak English, and not very well."

Max smiled as he looked at me in my mirror.

We pulled out of the airport parking lot and onto a six-lane road.

Kunming was more modern than I had expected. With high-rises in the distance, we drove past tall apartment buildings and shopping centers. Though it was a big city, it was green, lined with jacaranda trees and parks.

Six lanes became four lanes that turned into two as we left Kunming behind.

Green fields morphed to white, snowcapped mountains in the distance with fallow farmland and ancient tea trees along the roadside becoming the norm. We passed a donkey pulling an empty, weather-beaten wooden cart. An old man sat slumped; he held the reins in one hand and smoked a pipe in the other while his long, thin gray beard blew sideways in the breeze. Vin drove with a heavy foot, and the hypnotic rhythm of the van whizzing past vast open spaces made my eyelids heavy. I drifted off to sleep. When I woke, it was dusk in Lijiang.

With its red paper lanterns and fairy lights dangling from tree limbs, the town felt otherworldly. Two-story brick buildings stacked together with curved tiled rooftops while stone-paved streets lined with shops and residences bordered the narrow canals. We pulled into a two-story wooden building where Vin checked us into our rooms. I was so jet-lagged and emotionally spent I was just grateful it was a nice room with a clean bed. I couldn't wait to crawl under the covers and sleep. But first, food.

On our way to dinner we walked down the festive walkways. I peered in the small shops, noticing each had a specialty, from a tea shop, to a bead shop, to a scarf shop where the weaver sat at her loom. Massage signs in both English and Chinese pointed up staircases in between the shops and food establishments.

We passed a window display filled with vacuum-sealed food packages. Two labeled in English read YAK MEAT. A mini river filled with orange and white koi ran alongside the thoroughfare. A tiny bridge crossed over to a patio where we dined under a tree trimmed with twinkling lights. Despite my exhaustion, it was a magical evening.

The next day we traveled all morning through barren farm-land and tiered rice fields in remote mountains. Small farmhouses were few and far between on the two-lane road.

We drove for miles without seeing another car.

# 18

"WHAT'S THAT?" I POINTED TO A THREE-WHEELED CONTRAPTION darting down the street as we entered Nuodeng. It was half motorcycle, half golf cart, with a weathered off-white canvas-covered top forming a structure that separated the driver from his passengers—a very rough-and-ready form of a taxi. In the back sat a mother with two small children, and a live rooster on her lap stuck his neck out as they zipped past.

"Tuk-tuk," Vin said.

"Tuk-tuk," Max repeated.

The buildings were taller than Lijiang, three to five stories, and without Lijiang's Asian flair. Here, everything was a shade of gray. Two skinny dogs followed a woman carrying cloth bags filled with groceries.

"This is the new village of Nuodeng. Nuodeng proper is up there." Max pointed up to the top of the vast mountain in front of us. Red clay houses stacked on top of each other scattered up the hillside. "Vin says that's where we're shooting."

Our hotel was three stories tall with a hint of an upturned roof. On the front of the building a large fan with Chinese letters was etched in stone. Tall white tiles with ink drawings of trees, plants, and mountains framed the entrance.

"You finally made it," Eva shouted while Vin began unloading the van. "I know you want to get settled, so I'll make this quick."

We followed her into the office while she explained that the film crew had booked the whole hotel. My room, a suite on the third floor, was where Max and I would work. Just outside the office door, costumes were being moved from a hotel room next to us into a van in the parking lot. Directly across from that room was the outside staircase. Max stood beside me, waiting for his room assignment.

"I have some per diem for you." She fumbled through the papers on her desk. "There's no way for you to access cash in China unless you have an account with the Bank of China. You don't, do you?"

"No."

"There are no ATMs here. And they don't accept credit cards. It's all about cash. So watch your money carefully."

She handed me a sealed white envelope. "Robert's on set right now. We're having dinner tonight. Meet us here at seven."

I climbed the three flights of stairs and ambled down the exterior walkway until it ended at my room.

Room 311.

I turned the knob and swung open the door.

Daylight poured through an enormous picture window at the far end of the room.

It felt massive, so much bigger than the seat I had been assigned the past four days.

And it was mine.

All mine.

Giant panes of glass overlooked the main road. Directly across the street stood a building with a large neon sign. Tea trees as old as the hill they grew on framed the back of the building. Below, a donkey saddled with two empty, enormous straw baskets waited for his person. I watched tuk-tuks and cars whiz by below. It was grounding not to be in a moving vehicle of any kind.

There was a white leather sofa, blue carpeting with tiny yellow stars, and muted yellow drapes that framed both windows. The bedroom was compact with a queen-size bed, a tiny window above it, and a bedside table.

I had finally landed at my first location.

I threw myself on the bed. The mattress firm—just the way I liked it. My body tired, aching from all the bouncing around on uneven and ill-paved roads for the past two days.

And I missed Ron like crazy. The bed felt too big without him. Lying on my back, I moved my arms and legs back and forth as if I were making snow angels. Before I left LA, I was so worried about not being able to work without Ron by my side, I hadn't even thought about not waking up to that furry little face every morning.

But . . . I was about to edit a film.

*Not just any film.*

Cinderella.

*The original.*

*Not a copy.*

*Or a wannabe.*

*And I would see Robert tonight at dinner.*

*First time in years.*

*Robert's really stepping out—writing and directing his first feature film.*

*And to shoot it in a foreign country, in a foreign language.*

*While filming in rural locations in China along the Tibetan border.*

Each one of those, in itself, is a difficult, almost impossible task.

So to do them all on your own was either heroic or insane.

My heart began to race as I thought about cutting this film.

I never thought Robert would make this happen, yet here I was.

At the first location.

I'd worked on only a couple of feature films and always with another editor.

Never solo.

Never on my own.

I was going to be editing my first feature film on my own, in a language I didn't speak.

*In a land far, far away . . . really far, far away.*

# 19

mobile. He looked up at me, raising his eyebrows with a huge smile as a gust of cold wind blew through the passageway.

"You're here!" Robert gave me an enthusiastic hug.

"I am."

"Quite the trip, huh? Jet-lagged?"

"Severely."

"Looks like your equipment arrived, too. Just in time," he said, nodding toward the parking lot.

While the men checked luggage tags against a shipment inventory, Max stacked boxes and cases to the side. I pulled out my hot pink cashmere gloves from my coat pocket, feeling Ron's tennis ball as I did. I gave it a squeeze, wondering what he was doing at that moment, and then thought about the walks we would do after lunch at work where we canvassed the exterior of the city's public tennis courts. Every outing, Ron found a stray ball. His furry little legs strutted with such self-assured pride when he returned to the office with a new one to add to his collection.

Eva joined us, introducing a woman with a bob cut and a smile that lit up the dark hallway. "This is Sunny, our production coordinator."

"It's all here," Max said, rubbing his hands together, trying to get warm. "Vin is going to carry the equipment to your suite and I'll set it up in the morning."

"Well, come on, then. The restaurant's only a block from here," Robert said as we crossed the parking lot. Given his six-foot-two frame, his long legs had a wide stride, so it was a brisk walk. Dirt blew in my face while my hair flew into my eyes, making it hard to see where I was going. My body felt un-steady, not knowing what time of day it was.

At the corner, Robert stood below an exposed light bulb swaying in the flurry, holding open a wooden door. We walked up a flight of stairs where off-white subway tile lined the walls. At the top of the stairs, a narrow hallway opened into three small rooms. Eva led the way into one that housed a round table.

When Robert's phone rang, he grabbed the call and stepped back into the hallway.

Sunny, Max, and I took a seat while Eva spoke to our wait-ress. Eva had a take-charge kind of attitude about her. The kind that comes with being a good line producer. She was taller than me with long, straight black hair tied back in a ponytail. Brown wooden prayer beads wrapped her left wrist.

Robert walked back in and sat next to me.

"So, I'm sure Eva has gone over the schedule with you, but we are here in Nuodeng for the next four weeks. Then we travel to Shaxi for seven weeks and on to Stone City for two. There's room at the end of the schedule for a week of pickups." He rifled through the papers he'd brought. Pulling one out, he skimmed down the page, took a pen from his pocket, and made a note at the top.

The waitress arrived with a teapot of hot green tea, small

teacups, bowls, chopsticks, and a couple of beers. Sunny poured the tea. Robert and Max both grabbed their beers.

Robert continued with his usual enthusiasm, "I can't wait for you to see Shaxi. It was part of the southern Silk Road, so the history there is astounding. The square, where we are going to shoot the ball, has an old opera house with a temple built during the Ming Dynasty. There is an ancient tea tree in the center of the square. It's just perfect for our ball."

Eva pointed to each dish. "So we have steamed rice. Eggplant. Chicken. Fish. And green beans. Any special dietary concerns?" she asked as she looked at me.

"I don't eat chicken."

"Then steer clear of this one."

"Our last location is Stone City. It's an hour donkey ride down the mountain to the town. The rest of us will hike to the river and camp for the week. That's where we'll shoot all the water and rice field scenes." Robert carried on, spinning the lazy Susan, filling his bowl from each hot dish. "We're going to be able to show people a part of China that's so untouched. It's as if time has stood still in these places."

I'd seen a lot of Europe with old towns, castles, and bridges, but hearing Robert discuss the history of these places, with dynasties and Silk Roads, sounded so otherworldly. The locations just perfect for telling a fairy tale.

"You basically have the rest of the week to get acclimated. And then next week, we start shooting the first scene," he said as he put his empty bowl on the table and finished his beer. "Max ordered everything you'll need. He's going to take great care of you."

"Where are the napkins?" I asked.

Eva reached into her pocket and pulled out a packet of tissues and handed one to me.

Max looked over at me, holding his bowl under his chin, shoveling the rest of his noodles in his mouth, and smiled. I did my best to return the smile though I felt myself nodding like a bobblehead wanting to nod off to sleep.

"You and Max must go to the store tomorrow and pick up tissues, as they don't supply them anywhere here, restaurants or restrooms. And I recommend a heating pad. It's really cold at night," Eva suggested as she paid the waitress. "Robert, we need to go over the last few things you are going to need for the test tomorrow with Wang Lee."

Robert looked down at his phone, thumbed through a few buttons, stared at the screen, then at his watch, and then over at the window.

"Being the director, the decisions never end," he said with a smile as he looked at me. "You should come by the set tomorrow." He gathered his stack of pages, giving the top page a glance before looking at me again. "Really glad you're here, Lisa. We're gonna make a great movie."

# 20

"GOOD MORNING," MAX COUGHED, NOT LOOKING UP FROM the monitors, startling me.

I ran back into my bedroom, slipped on a pair of sweatpants and a sweater, and entered the room again.

"Take two. *Good morning, Max.*"

"Good morning."

For the first time, he looked up at me and smiled.

I searched around for the electric kettle—it stood alone on the table.

Now for a mug and tea bags. I opened the drawers below.

"Max, do you know where I might find a mug and some tea?"

"We need to go to the store today. The hotel does not supply either of them."

*Oh shit! No tea!*

All three monitors stood in place, the mixing board with its microphone hooked up and ready to go. My keyboard, trackball, and settings all loaded. Even my wrist pads were in their place.

Max was quick on the keyboard. Confident as he hit each key. I could already tell I was lucky to be working with him.

"And there was footage to be loaded, so I'm taking care of

that now. Robert invited us to the set and I wanna see what's going on, so Vin and I are going in a few minutes. Wanna join us?"

"Yes. I would love to go. I'm going to make a quick phone call first."

I closed the door to the bedroom and opened the curtains. I wasn't sure how many days it had been since I'd seen Ron, but I crawled back into bed, opened my laptop, adjusted the pillows behind my back, and hit Mavis's number. It rang and rang and rang and rang. She didn't pick up. My heart sank. I'd have to try again later.

# 21

OUR HIKE TO THE OLD VILLAGE OF NUODENG WOVE UP AND around the mountain. Crimson-red houses with tubular tiled rooftops tucked deep into the clay-colored hillside. Small green patches dusted the terrain, but terra cotta was the local color.

The trail grew narrower as the incline grew steeper. Piles of boulders had been placed along the side to keep the pathway clear of mudslides. Red clay bricks of different shapes and sizes made small houses that lined the trail. Cracks and fallen plaster gave me the feeling that people had been living up here a long time, weathering the elements, walking this narrow path bringing food, firewood, and life's necessities each day to their hillside homes. We passed through an alleyway with stairs so narrow and steep only one person could pass through at a time. A small stream ran down one side of the mountain. Very little water flowed from it, making me think it hadn't rained much this year.

After we had hiked farther up the mountain, I had a chance to look out and could see the valley of New Nuodeng below and the tall mountains that surrounded it. I could even see our hotel on the edge of town.

Around the bend, a large staircase appeared.

Here, there was no incline.

It went straight up the side of the mountain.

Constructed out of concrete, the stairs were uneven in height and depth.

And there were at least fifty of them.

Vin stood at the top, the sun reflecting off each jumbo anvil case he carried.

I thought how the crew would be hiking this every day.

Some more than once a day.

And for four weeks.

I glanced up at the daunting endeavor, when coming down the staircase appeared a woman twice my age. With cotton slippers on her feet and a bounce in her step, she lugged a bag of rice the size of a sixth grader on her back. I sat on the side of one of the wide steps and watched her maneuver her way down the rocky staircase like a gymnast performing her routine at the Olympics.

Max waved from the top stair and waited for me.

"Did you see that woman with the rice bag?" I huffed and puffed.

"I took her photo," he said while he studied me. "You need to rest."

Max sat next to me on a boulder between the staircase and the mountain and we looked down at the rooftops of all the houses we had passed on the way up. A hundred of them—the incline so steep, making it nearly impossible to distinguish one domicile from the next.

We were higher up now, giving me a much wider view of New Nuodeng and the area that surrounded it. I could see now that the small green patches scattered on the flat parts of the mountain were modest farm fields. The rest of the mountains were covered in aged brown, naked bushes and trees, looking as if they had lived there a long time—longer than the houses, longer than the old people who walked this mountain every day. We watched an old man with a donkey trudge up the mountain, enormous cinder blocks strapped to each side of the donkey's body. He moved slow and steady, not missing a step, not needing to rest.

*This is going to be my one and only time to the set. And I'm never going to start my day again without caffeine.*

We rounded the last corner of the trail where it spilled into a large plateau with a vista point of endless mountains as far as I could see. They stood like old warriors, strong and noble against the cobalt-blue sky with transit clouds. A horseshoe courtyard overlooked this spectacular view with an ancient, colossal stone gate, providing the entrance into the lost-in-time village where the crew would be shooting for the next month.

# 22

HE HANDED ME A COKE. IT WAS WARM, NOT THE WAY I LIKED IT,
but I was hoping the sugar would pick me up.

"Five yuan," Max said.

I dug into my coat pocket and found my per diem envelope.

"Lunch will be served by the guesthouse over there." He
pointed to a courtyard near another building. Three women
scurried around moving enormous pots among several tables.
"You need to carry your own snacks. We will go shopping after
lunch."

We sat on a bench under a covered patio while locals stood
around smoking cigarettes, watching forty small children—ex-
tras—being wrangled by three women. They were instructing
them for the shoot the next day. Most of them sat under the
shade of a gnarly old tree, but four feral tykes chased each other
around, squealing and laughing. All dressed in their costumes of
long tunics and wide pants in shades of indigo and gray. Each
head topped with a hat. They looked to be about four or five, the
age of our Cinderella, our little Mei Mei, when she loses her
mother.

I waved. "*Nǐ hǎo.*"

A few smiled at me—their teeth all shapes and sizes. But

mostly they stared. One little girl sported pigtails that stood straight out to the side—her bottom jaw dropped so low it almost hit her chest. A little boy missing two front teeth gawked at me hard, never once blinking. I'm not sure any of these children had ever seen a blond-haired, green-eyed woman before.

One brave soul, a fairy girl with bright red, pudgy cheeks and a runny nose, stood up and shouted, "*Nǐ hǎo!*"

Across from the courtyard, beneath an old overhang, I spotted the camera. Behind it, a man donning a gray checkered flat cap peered through the lens. He pointed to the lights and skims. Two men flanked the camera while others moved around the set, making adjustments.

"That's Wang Lee in the hat," Max said. "When they break for lunch, I will introduce you."

Robert entered the set like a mother duck crossing the road with her babies, only Robert's ducklings were all juggling things. First in line, a woman wearing a full-length black pin-striped apron carrying several garments in her hands with something beaded dangling over her shoulder. A thin short man juggled a lantern, a candlestick, and a torch as he ran alongside, trying to keep up with Robert's long strides. Bringing up the rear was a young girl in jeans, a T-shirt, and a bomber jacket with an open script in one hand and a pen in the other.

We watched as the crew flurried about preparing for the next day, while Vin told us that the old village was famous for its salt wells and a temple, until they broke for lunch.

# 23

"WHAT DO YOU THINK?" ROBERT SHOUTED AS WE WALKED toward the camera crew. "Great set, huh?"

"Extraordinary. Just magical."

"No need for set dressing," he said with a huge smile before a man carrying a tall pole distracted him.

We passed men building things, children having their costumes inspected, and locals smoking while watching the show of it all until we reached under the eaves of one of the guesthouses where the camera crew gathered, having just finished their lunch. A man who wasn't much taller than me, in a black down vest, jeans, and hiking boots, stood in front of me. He rubbed his clean-shaven head before covering it in a gray flannel flat cap.

"This is Wang Lee," Max said as I held out my hand.

"Hello," Wang Lee said, nodding as he shook my hand.

"*Nǐ hǎo*, Wang Lee. So nice to meet you!"

He looked me in the eyes and smiled.

Max and I waited for him to respond. When he didn't, Max interpreted what I said again.

Wang Lee nodded, then he spoke in Mandarin.

There was a sweetness in his delivery that made me relax. His voice was soft and thoughtful while his brown eyes and smile sparked with joy and enthusiasm.

"He says, 'So honored to meet a big-time Hollywood editor with so much experience.'"

I smiled, having never heard "honored" or "big-time" said about me before.

"Tell him how honored I am to work with a big-time Chinese cinematographer."

Max translated.

Wang Lee blushed, then nodded, excused himself, and went back to work.

Max, Vin, and I hung around a little longer to watch them shoot a couple of test shots with our little Mei Mei (Cinderella) who followed the direction given to her with grace and ease. She appeared quiet and reserved in between takes. She was a sharp contrast to the many Hollywood child actors I had observed on sets who had tantrums when gummy bears were served instead of gummy snakes and used four-letter words not becoming of five-year-olds.

We stopped to take in one last look at the grand view before we began the trek back down. The picturesque mountains stood tall amongst the clouds with the enchanting village behind us. The sun disappeared, causing the temperature to drop quickly. I stopped to put on my gloves, zip up my coat, and wrap my scarf around my neck. As we descended that vertical staircase, I had to hold on to the side of the wall each step of the way down.

# 24

"WE ARE GOING SHOPPING AS PROMISED," MAX SAID AS VIN dropped us off. It looked like a general store of sorts. Max held the door open for me while I stepped inside, giving a jangle to brass bells that hung from the door.

Shelves lined the shop from floor to ceiling, from the front of the store all the way to the back, with barely enough room to walk in between.

I followed Max down the shoe aisle. A very small selection of women's slip-ons. Some might call them scuffs or slippers at home in the States. These were made from mesh or cotton. In bright reds and greens with beaded flowers and Chinese characters.

On the bottom two rungs, plastic men's slippers were displayed.

I continued down the aisle to kitchenware. Dishes stacked in two patterns, white or red with yellow Chinese characters. An array of plastic chopsticks in a variety of colors filled boxes. Tiny glass cups without handles sat next to glass teapots.

"Lisa, over here. I found the thermoses."

Max had already chosen a blue one. I chose silver.

"We need tea. What kind do you like?"

"Jasmine."

I grabbed several packages of tissues while Max dropped off his items at the checkout desk before looking for the heating pads.

"Found them," he said.

A petite lady wearing a yellow rain hat stood behind the counter. She wrote down the price on a piece of paper as she carried on in Mandarin. Max nodded and paid her, placing his items in a bright yellow cloth bag.

"*Nǐ hǎo*," I said, smiling as I reached for my per diem.

When all the items had been added up, she looked at me as if she'd added *me* up, and said something.

Max began speaking to her.

The shop owner stared up at me, with her hand out.

I looked at her hand and then to Max.

"Sixty-five yuan."

I opened my per diem envelope, rummaged through the bills, and handed her a hundred-yen bill. She snapped the crisp paper before shooting one last stern look at me. She reached over, punched a button that opened her cash drawer, and counted out the change into my hand. Then she looked back up at me and said something with a no-nonsense expression.

"She's giving us the bags for free. But next time, she's gonna charge us, so we better bring it back when we shop here again."

"*Shay shay*," I said as I pointed to the bag she had just gifted me.

It was cold. The adrenaline that had kicked in at the beginning of our shopping had vanished. It took everything I had to put one foot in front of the other. Max walked beside me in silence.

When we reached the hotel and I began the walk up my flight of stairs, I turned to Max. "I'm gonna lie down for a bit."

# 25

IT WAS THE MIDDLE OF THE NIGHT AND I FELT WIDE AWAKE.

Missing Ron, I closed my eyes, rubbed the open space on the bed next to me, and made a wish for him to magically appear.

I squeezed my eyes tight . . . to give him that extra boost of energy to get all the way to Yunnan.

And then . . .

I opened my eyes.

The bed was still empty.

I was alone, on my own. Wishing for something wasn't going to change it, so I got up and showered.

The hot water soothed the ache in my calves.

I crawled back into bed with my new heating pad on high and thought about my day. The excruciating hike up the mountain. The chaos on top as the film crew prepared for the first day of shooting. People rushing to and fro saying things I couldn't understand.

It all felt a bit like my life.

I'd taken this job, been so busy getting ready to get here, I had no time to think any of it through.

*Was this even something I could do?*

It was certainly something I had never done before, run off to nowhere, China, to join a movie crew.

A crew that didn't speak English.

Not one word.

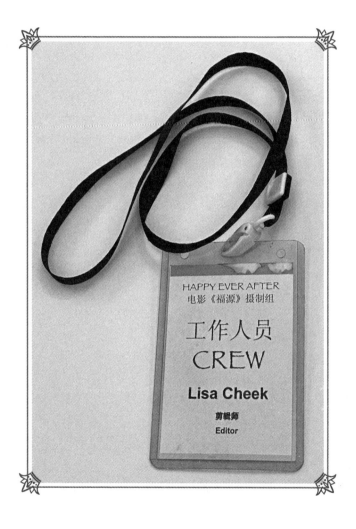

# 26

DAYLIGHT POURED THROUGH THE MINI WINDOW. GRATEFUL that I didn't have to show up the first day of shooting . . . grateful that I didn't have to climb that monster . . . scale that behemoth . . . all the way to the top.

*Once a Valley girl, always a Valley girl.*

# 27

Thoroughly exhausted, I could barely keep my eyelids open. But when I tried to . . . I couldn't help but think about Ron Howard . . . my heart ached . . . my eyelids were heavy . . . so heavy . . . and . . . before I knew it . . .

Skype rang.

"Ron."

"Mavis."

"Lisa?"

Mavis leaned into her computer, giving me a view up her nostrils.

"Are you there?"

"I'm here! I'm here!" I shouted.

"I can't hear you," Mavis said as she zoomed out to a wide shot. She was sitting in her bed, leaning up against a shabby-chic white wicker headboard in a floral nightgown with a high ruffled collar. She took an awkward drag off a cigarette and blew it into the screen, vanishing into the smoke.

"I'm so glad you called."

"There's been . . . and . . . when . . ."

"Mavis. You're cutting out. And what the hell happened to your eye?"

Her left eye was the size of a full-grown grapefruit and every shade of purple.

"...so...then...he..."

"Something is wrong with our connection!"

"And then...well...I...and you know..."

Sugar Ray walked into the frame, sat next to Mavis, and looked into the camera, his snout giving a big snort.

"Mavis, you look like you've been in a terrible accident. Where's Ron?"

"I tried to..."

She raised her right hand in full view of the camera, as if motioning to something. I was hoping it was Ron.

It was her arm, covered in a hard plaster cast.

All the way past her elbow.

"I need to see Ron. I need to see Ron. I need to see Ron," I pleaded.

The computer screen went black, and a man in a suit with a handheld microphone appeared.

"Breaking news. Early this morning on 17th and Wilshire in Santa Monica, a German shepherd attacked a small dog. According to several witnesses, it appears the victim, who we have just identified as Ron Howard, allegedly started the confrontation. That's all the details we have right now. Jack Jones for Channel Four."

"I'm here! I'm here, Ron Howard!" I screamed, waking myself from a deep sleep.

I glanced over at the clock.

2:37 a.m.

Fucking jet lag.

# 28

I OPENED MY COMPUTER.

*Ring.*

*Ring.*

*Ring.*

*Ring.*

Her camera appeared, several limbs flayed, and a tail passed through.

"Lisa?"

"Mavis!"

"Hang on. Let me get this phone so you can see everyone."

The image went from upside down to sideways. There were sounds of barking and knocking things over and something rubbing against something else. Sounds of sniffing grew louder. And there, on the corner of the sofa, I could see Ron's teddy bear body standing on the sofa, marching in place, with his tail wagging like a flag on a windy day.

"Ron. I'm here. Can you see me?"

His tail wagged faster and faster but it was clear he didn't know where to look.

"Look, Ron Howard! She's right here in this little box!"

Mavis's finger filled the screen. I could hear Ron barking,

but I couldn't tell if the bark was anxious or eager. Whatever it was, this must have been confusing for him.

"How's the trip?"

"Long, but I'm at the first location. I've been trying to call you." I pulled the duvet up around my shoulders.

"We've been here. The boys watch episodes of *Snapped* all day while I write my piece on celebrities' fall from fame."

"I had an awful nightmare—you aren't having any trouble with the German shepherds, are you?"

"Haven't seen a one. We're all just fine. Peachy! A party every day." Mavis reached for a cigarette as Ron came back into view. "He missed you for the first few days, but he's settled in now." She patted him on the head. "The three of us all sleep together in my bed. It's quite cozy."

"I miss him so much. It's a bigger adjustment than I thought."

"You'll be fine. He'll be fine. It's dinnertime for us here."

"Hold him up to the screen. I want to see his face."

Mavis disappeared and Ron reappeared. I reminded him to be a good boy and assured him I'd call again. My heart ached for a snuggle with my guy.

The call ended as quickly as it began and I was once again alone.

It was cold outside. I was sad but I felt safe in my new bed.

*When I was four, my father finished his master's degree at UNC Chapel Hill in world affairs, and he got his first job as an engineer in Worcester, Massachusetts. He and Mommy rented a little duplex*

on a sheep farm outside of Rudland in the middle of nowhere. We didn't have any neighbors.

There wasn't another child in sight.

I entertained myself with Disney records. Cinderella was my favorite. I listened to "A Dream Is a Wish Your Heart Makes" over and over again while I plugged pegs into my Lite-Brite. I had a whole slew of stuffed animals and spent my days dreaming they came to life, playing and talking to me.

They comforted me when Mommy and Daddy fought.

They watched over me while I slept.

They kept my secret of feeling scared that Mommy was going to leave Daddy and take me with her.

And then when I turned five, she did—and we moved in with her parents in Miami.

In a two-bedroom apartment on the third floor overlooking the ocean.

Mommy got a job working at the Eden Roc hotel.

My English Gran and Swedish Papa babysat me.

Many years ago when Gran first moved to the States, she worked at Macy's in Manhattan and married a man who was later committed to a mental hospital.

Papa was a lawyer. His first wife committed suicide and homicide: he came home one day to find the oven gas turned on—she and the baby dead in the kitchen.

While he was in a haze of grief and unconvention, his second wife proposed to him before a monthlong excursion to Sweden only to divorce him two months later in Reno.

Gran was Papa's third wife. They never celebrated a wedding anniversary and wouldn't tell anyone when it was. Rumor has it, Mommy and her younger brother were born before they got married—and they got married only because Papa's law firm told him he needed to do the right thing—but none of that was ever verified by either party.

Mommy and I left Daddy in a hurry—packing only one suitcase—so one day Gran took me to Neiman Marcus and bought me a stuffed cocker spaniel to comfort me. I named her Lulu.

I spent my days dancing in the living room with Papa while he sang Swedish songs. Once, I accidentally broke a bird statue my uncle made in ceramics class. When he came home from boarding school and saw what I had done, he threatened to throw me off the balcony of the three-story apartment building.

I missed Daddy.

Mommy and Daddy got married because she was pregnant with me.

She was twenty.

He was twenty-two.

They were kids themselves.

But at five, I felt like I had to be the grown-up.

I never saw Mommy now.

Daddy wouldn't send Mommy any money and she couldn't make it on her own.

So we went back—because Daddy promised he would take a new job . . . in Johannesburg, South Africa.

# 29

EDITING A MOVIE IS NOT LIKE EDITING A COMMERCIAL. A commercial is thirty seconds and can be completed in a couple of days. It's about grabbing your attention.

A feature is a test of perseverance. You're in it for the long haul. It's a marathon; it's ninety minutes, or two hours, of a story that needs to make sense—it has to have a beginning, a middle, and an end.

It was a new day, but I still felt uneasy.

Three monitors stared blankly back at me and provided no wisdom, no reassurance.

*Well, I'm here. Now what?* Thinking, thinking . . . thinking . . .

I walked back into the bedroom, hung up some clothes, and unpacked a few more things. Sent a couple of emails, but the internet was slow, so much slower than what I was used to. Posting a photo to social media took forever, so I posted only two photos: Max and I sitting on the big boulder together and the one Max took of me once at the top, overlooking New Nuodeng.

Once the photos were up, I waited, hoping to make contact with someone I knew.

But not even *one* like.

It was 2009. Facebook was in its infancy, not like it is now, and the internet in this rural village in China was suspect.

I wondered if my Facebook account was being scrutinized the way my passport had been, by some man in a tall glass cage wearing a military uniform, clicking through my photos and posts—checking to see who I had poked.

Remember that button? Being poked? Who was the genius who thought of that interaction?

BTW ("by the way" for those who don't use acronyms), I never poked anyone.

# 30

IT WAS DARK BY THE TIME MAX ARRIVED. HE HOOKED UP THE dailies to load into our machine and then handed me a cup of instant noodles.

"I figured you might be hungry."

"You figured right. Thank you."

"I got you the vegetable one."

*He remembers that I don't eat chicken.*

"So how did the first day go?" I asked.

"It was great! My first time on a set!" He beamed with excitement. "They need me the rest of the week."

Their gain, my loss. "You won't be here? Editing with me?"

"It's just until things settle down up there."

We watched the footage load into the computer. It was shots of the children we'd seen the day before watching a shadow puppet show.

"They didn't get all the setups slated for today, so we are already behind." Max slurped his noodles, a sound I wasn't fond of.

"The contrast in lighting—the way it highlights their precious porcelain faces—are angelic—so enchanting," I commented.

I turned from the screen to Max, his face half-buried in the

Cup O' Noodles. "I had a late start today, but I'd like to have breakfast with you tomorrow morning."

"Okay, I'll meet you out front at six," Max said as he hooked up the last drive before he left for the night.

# 31

IT WAS STILL DARK AS WE CROSSED THE DESERTED STREET AND entered a massive warehouse with thirty-foot-high ceilings and no heat. Four long tables with benches filled with people eating breakfast. A pigeon sat next to a busted window.

Max stopped in front of a large, deep, stainless-steel pot, lifted the lid, and stirred the contents.

"Congee," he said with a proud smile as he showed it to me. "May I get you a bowl?"

"What is it?"

"Boiled rice."

"A small scoop, please."

I felt like Oliver Twist with his portion of porridge.

"What are those?" I asked, pointing to a stack of white round rolls, as we walked down the buffet table—if you can even call it that with its meager assortment of items.

"Sticky buns."

"But they don't look like they've been baked."

"They steam the dough in a wok."

*I want my blueberry muffin.*

"Any salt and pepper for the congee or jam and butter to go on the sticky bun?"

"Sometimes they serve pickles with the congee, but our server said they ran out this morning. The buns we eat plain."

Steam rose from my bowl of blandness.

I was hungry and the congee was hot. I dove in. It tasted like rice and water—exactly what it is.

The sticky bun was not sticky with sweetness. Its blandness rivaled the congee.

Max held the bowl close to his mouth—the spoon never far from the bowl.

I fantasized about a cup of coffee.

*A young, cute barista with a Hollywood smile packing the grounds into the basket.*

*Hot almond milk frothed to perfection.*

*The warm cup between my hands as I take my first sip of the day.*

"Ready to go?" Max interrupted while I was still daydreaming about coffee and the barista.


The early morning light arrived, waking up the village.

A young man on an old moped drove by as I spotted a tuk-tuk parked at the end of the road. An old woman hopped in the driver's seat and darted off while Max sprinted toward the mountain. "I'll see you with more footage tonight."

I went back to my room and called Mavis.

She didn't pick up.

Out of loneliness, I looked at the photos of Ron on my computer. In one, he was sitting in a director's chair on a set. His hair long. Curly poodle ringlets grew around his neck. It was so thick in this photo, he looked as if he were wearing an Elizabethan collar. His big brown eyes and black nose, long thin strands of hair flopping over the front of his pointed bear ears.

I took a big breath in and let it out.

Black empty screens sat on my desk.

It started to sink in deeper: I was doing this job on my own.

I began to feel overwhelmed by the size of the project.

I was going to have to tell a story, make it entertaining.

In Chinese!

*How do you say OH MY FUCKING GOD in Mandarin?*

I couldn't breathe.

I started hyperventilating—gasping for air.

I felt as if I were drowning.

When I was seven and we were living in Johannesburg, we spent our Christmas in Durban, South Africa. I thought it was strange to go to the beach at Christmas because in Massachusetts we had three feet of snow when Santa came.

One afternoon, I went for a swim.

The day was gray.

Cold.

The beach didn't have sand here. It had rocks—lots and lots of rocks.

The tide was rough.

The undertow strong.

I was tired and wanted to get out, to go rest on the beach, but the waves knocked me down.

*Kept pulling me under.*

*Exhausted, I screamed, "Mommy!"*

*Coughing.*

*Water in my lungs.*

*The undertow under again.*

*Salt water up my nose.*

*"Help!"*

*Everything was blurry.*

*"Daddy!"*

*My feet reached toward the bottom, but the rocks were slippery.*

*I was swallowed up—pulled farther away from the beach.*

*Out into deeper and deeper water.*

*My feet no longer touched the bottom.*

*I'm scared.*

*I can't hold my breath any longer.*

*A stranger grabbed me around the waist and took me out of the water, laid me on the ground, and gave me mouth-to-mouth resuscitation.*

*Where are Mommy and Daddy?*

# 32

I TRIED MAVIS AGAIN.

"Everything okay?"

"Lonely. Missing Ron."

"Give it time. You'll make friends." Mavis rubbed night cream in her cheek. "We're off to sleep."

"Can I see Ron in the frame for me?"

Mavis moved her phone so I could see Ron and Sugar Ray curled up at the foot of her bed.

"Love you, Ron." I waited for him to look up . . . but he didn't.

I needed to get out.

There was a quiet hum—sounds of distant car engines, the occasional squeak of tuk-tuk wheels, a murmur of low voices. With my hand in my pocket holding tight to Ron's tennis ball, I passed through the empty parking lot and watched the wind blow one dried-up leaf with holes in it tumbling across the tarmac. The empty parking lot led to the main street, where the lone leaf landed in a pile of rubbish.

Across the road stood a small portable stall.

A woman dressed in a red down coat restocked her shelves.

On her countertop, in the corner, sat a gold lucky cat waving its left arm.

Behind her, tied to the chain-link fence, sat a small black and brown puppy.

"*Nǐ hǎo*," I greeted the shopkeeper with a smile.

She looked at me, gave me the once-over, pursing her lips . . . then she went back to stocking her stall.

"*Nǐ hǎo*," I repeated while I walked closer to the puppy, who was now jumping up and down, pulling on the fence. "May I pet your dog?"

Nothing. She didn't respond.

The puppy's butt started to wiggle faster while her tail tapped the dirt, dust flying everywhere, covering my tennis shoes. I got down on my knees, leaned in, and rubbed the little girl's face with both hands.

She squealed with excitement.

"You are the cutest!"

She had the markings of a black and brown German shepherd, but her paws were small so she was not going to be anywhere near that size, likely no bigger than Ron. She stared at me with her big black eyes while she stood up on her hind legs. The rope around her neck barely had a two-foot lead, so I moved in as close to her as I could, finally sitting down in the dirt, crossing my legs so she could jump into my lap and we could watch the world go by together.

With my back against the chain-link fence, I watched the shopkeeper, now stacking cups of noodles next to the lucky cat while the little pup's tiny teeth gnawed on my fingers.

An old man—long silver beard down to his waist—approached. The shopkeeper placed a pack of cigarettes on the counter. He handed her a few yuan. Words were exchanged before he looked over at me soaking up the sun, then he turned back at her.

He said something.

Their faces scrunched up, looking as if they'd just smelled rotten eggs.

It was such a small village.

I wondered how they knew each other.

If they knew each other.

They must have known each other.

*Her brother?*

*Next-door neighbor?*

*Did he leave her at the altar?*

I stroked my new friend's back. She looked up at me. Her expressive eyes sparkled like black diamonds in the sunlight.

Two toddlers, holding on to their mother's coat hem, approached the stall. She spoke with the shopkeeper and they made their exchange as one child yanked on her mother's pant leg to be picked up. The mother swooped her up in her arms with the bag of new purchases, and the three were on their way with the older child turning around, her eyes never leaving me until they disappeared around a corner.

It felt good to be outside in the fresh air, snuggling with this furry little girl who seemed to be enjoying my company as much as I enjoyed hers, but I needed to stretch my legs and get some exercise.

"I'll be back soon," I promised as I dusted off my clothes.

She cried as she tugged at the fence trying to follow me, but her rope was too short, making her land on her backside. I hated leaving her there, tied up, and unable to go for a walk with me. She whimpered. I had to stop looking back.

# 33

I FELT ON DISPLAY WHILE I WANDERED DOWN THE STREET ALONE.
When I walked with Ron, everyone was so enamored with him.

I felt exposed now, almost naked, without him by my side.

Gold Chinese characters painted on a large glass window caught my attention, so I peered in. Two wooden tables with chairs filled the pint-sized room. An old man in brown polyester pants with a bright blue dress coat sat alone, smoking a cigarette. As the cigarette came to an end, he lit another.

The chef, a woman, worked over two small burners next to the table. In one wok she cracked an egg and fried it. In the other, she added chopped garlic into hot oil. Once the garlic browned, she added vegetables, cooked rice, and soy sauce and spooned it up in a bowl. Added the fried egg on top and served it to her chain-smoking customer. He smoked while he ate and drank a tiny cup of tea.

Motorbikes, packed sardine style, lined the driveway of the next business. Handlebars, tires, seats, and engines lay among the two-wheel transportation depot, like an emergency waiting room, all in need of diagnosis before surgery could take place.

The next street I wandered down, I found myself in the middle of a farmers' market. Vendors laid out their goods on the ground on sheets and small tables.

Mounds of clementine oranges in bright, wrinkly skins with stems and leaves still attached appeared just picked.

Long red chiles were stacked beside them.

Tall white bags filled with potatoes, bok choy, and carrots stood next to each other.

A toothless woman in a quilted brown zip-up jacket with a matching brown crocheted hat sat behind a table of dried noodles and tofu in a bowl of water.

Farther down, tea leaves sprawled out on two tabletops.

Large bags of rice piled high on display.

Baby chicks filled wired cages.

A shopper in a navy-blue striped business suit, chatting on a mobile, picked up a small chick and put it on top of her shopping bag.

Cotton candy being spun in a rusted bath pan sat atop a rickety wooden stand. Children queued, ready to devour the sugary floss.

The street widened, opening up to an eating area, filled with tiny grills, each cooking their specialty. Chicken on skewers. Potatoes and turnips. Carrots and corn.

I looked all around, taking in the smell of grilled meat. The sounds of seared fat on high flames. The clacking of Mandarin. I watched people carrying heavy cloth bags filled with fresh produce.

Taking one last look before I headed out, I spotted the friendly face of a familiar woman sitting on a bench.

"*Nǐ hǎo.*"

"So happy to see you." Sunny, the film's production coordinator, beamed.

"So happy to see you."

I took a good look at the food item she gnawed on. It looked like a bird's foot, talons and all.

"It's delicious. Want some?" Sunny asked.

"No. No, thank you. I would definitely NOT want some." I studied each nail on its toe. They were long, in need of a trim.

"Okay. Come have a seat." She scooted over, making space for me on her bench.

I sat beside her and watched as she devoured the chicken foot, one phalange at a time.

"Sunny, would you be willing to teach me something in Mandarin?"

She licked her lips and wiped her fingers clean. "Yes. I would like that very much." She smiled as her eyes lit up like sparklers while she pondered what to teach me. "Ah. *Wǒ gǎndào hěn kāixīn*," she said.

"*Wǒ gǎndào hěn kāixīn*." I did my best to repeat what she said.

She giggled. "*Wǒ gǎndào hěn kāixīn*," she said very slowly.

"*Wǒ gǎndào hěn kāixīn*," I repeated back to her, hoping I was hitting the right tones.

"Hummmmmm?" she said, chuckling.

"What does it mean?"

"I am happy to see you."

"*Wǒ gǎndào hěn kāixīn*, Sunny."

"*Wǒ gǎndào hěn kāixīn*. It needs work, but I must go now."

"I'll walk with you."

We crossed the square.

"Your English is very good."

"Thank you." She lowered her head as she smiled from my compliment.

We walked over the small bridge that covered the little stream that ran through the tiny town. I saw a woman in the back of a tuk-tuk with her shopping bags piled so high all I could see was her frizzy gray hair and two big brown eyes staring out at me.

When we reached the production office on the ground floor, I felt a wave of exhaustion hit me as I practiced one more time. *"Wǒ gǎndào hěn kāixīn,* Sunny."

*"Wǒ gǎndào hěn kāixīn."*

# 34

I WOKE UP IN THE MIDDLE OF THE NIGHT, ALL MY CLOTHES STILL ON.

Max had left a note on the table under another cup of instant noodles.

*Did not want to wake you. Loaded all the dailies from today. We shoot the dialogue tomorrow, so you can begin to cut the scene. See you tomorrow night.*

I checked my emails, and I called Mavis—who didn't answer—and then uploaded my photos from the market. Since everyone was asleep, I had the entire village bandwidth to myself and was able to upload all ten photos. It still took almost an hour, but it's not like I had anything else to do.

I walked back into the office, took my seat in front of the monitors, and loaded a roll of film from the first day's shoot. It was of the children I had seen on the mountain. They were sitting on little stools, dressed in shades of indigo, sporting silver cuffs in organic shapes around their necks that glistened in the light.

I began to make a select roll, pulling my favorite shots:

A close-up of a boy smiling.

A medium shot of our little Mei Mei, concerned.

Another where she looked happy. A close-up where she looked sad.

I pulled a wide shot of the children sitting in their chairs, giving us the scope of the tiny room, and then a pan as the camera scanned the three rows of children.

I pulled a two-shot of a little boy with a runny nose sitting next to a little girl straightening her hat.

It felt good to start working.

The film was beautiful, the costumes and locations magical.

I loaded a reel from today's dailies.

These were of the shadow puppets—exotic and intricate . . .

One of the sun.

One of the moon.

One of a boy, the other of a girl.

I opened the script and matched the best takes of the puppets to the story in the script.

*I can do this.*

*I'm gonna be fine, just fine.*

*Lonely maybe, but fine.*

It was daylight by the time I finished, so I walked across the street and had breakfast . . . alone.

Same boring fare.

I took a seat at the end of a table away from the other diners.

No one sat beside me.

The isolation brought back old feelings of not fitting in, not being good enough, and being unlovable.

*Sitting alone on the bus.*

*Eating lunch alone.*

*No one to play with at recess.*

*Four different elementary schools . . .*

*First and second grade—Johannesburg, South Africa.*

*Third grade, first half—back to Chapel Hill, North Carolina.*

*Third grade, second half, fourth and fifth—Grosse Pointe Woods, Michigan.*

*Sixth grade—Newton, North Carolina.*

*Just when I made a friend, it was time to move.*

I felt no need to linger on these memories in a public place, so I went back to my room. My phone rang.

"Sorry I haven't made it to screen dailies with you." It was Robert on the other end. "It seems we are behind before we got started. How do they look?"

"Stunning. Extraordinary." It felt good to be talking to him.

"Great. You are my eyes. Send me selects and cuts when you can."

"I will."

"I need Max here on the set as much as possible right now."

I looked at Max's empty chair beside me.

"Oh, and one of our producers is coming to town. He's going to want to see the dailies. Don't show him anything unless I'm there . . . okay?"

"I won't."

Silence filled the empty room. Doing commercials, there were always people around. I could shut the door to my office if I wanted to be alone. But Moe and Stella were always there. And my assistant was never on the set. There were other editors and clients—someone to talk to.

And I had Ron Howard.

# 35

The picture was blurred, but I caught a snippet of a lit cigarette in an ashtray, then the sleeve of a hot pink terry cloth robe. The camera finally settled on Mavis. Green goop covered her face. The whites of her eyes peered into the lens.

"On your way out, I see."

"I knew you'd be calling and I wanted to look my best." Mavis chuckled as she adjusted the collar on her robe while she looked at herself in the camera. "There, that's better. So how's it going?"

"I wanna see Ron. I miss him."

She turned her laptop around to her feet.

"Hi, sweet boy. I miss you."

Ron looked over at Mavis, tilting his head to one side.

"I'm here. In the screen."

His triangle ears turned like a satellite dish fine-tuning its signal.

"Your boy's a genius, but I'm not sure he gets looking into the computer screen just yet." Mavis turned the screen back on her. She was now sporting a yellow turban on her head. "So what's on the docket today?"

"Waiting for more footage to arrive."

A timer went off in the background.

"Time's up—I gotta get this mask off. Wish me luck—I have to look twenty-one by tomorrow."

"I love you, Ron Howard."

"He loves you, too."

Mavis knew I needed to hear that.

And with that, the screen turned black.

# 36

I TRAIPSED TOWARD THE PRODUCTION OFFICE FOR SOME company. Sunny looked up from her phone. She smiled and waved while she chatted to the person on the other end. The copier spit out sheets and sheets of paper. On top of the table were scripts in Mandarin. I hadn't seen one of those before. Amazing. I studied the characters. The way a thin and fat line were connected. How each stroke stood out against the white of the page. They looked so difficult to duplicate. Was this one a word or a letter?

*I wonder how long it takes to master this intricate language— so beautiful but so confusing all at once.*

I watched Eva sporting her headset and wondered if she slept in that thing.

I waited for her to look up and notice me, but she was deep in conversation.

They had work to do, no time for me.

I headed out across the parking lot. Tuk-tuks darted back and forth while mopeds zipped by as I crossed the street over to the same vendor's stall I'd visited the day before.

The shopkeeper hustled her wares to a woman with a baby strapped to her back with a blanket. The puppy, still tied to the fence, danced on her hind legs, whining. The shopkeeper gave me a quick glance, still chatting with her customer.

"*Nǐ hǎo,*" I said through a smile, as I passed the two women on my way toward the dog. Her tail-wagging caused a large dust cloud.

I leaned in closer.

"*Wǒ gǎndào hěn kāixīn,*" I practiced as I petted her. "*Wǒ gǎndào hěn kāixīn.*"

I took my seat up against the fence and she jumped in my lap.

The shopkeeper walked toward me until she was standing directly over me.

"*Wǒ gǎndào hěn kāixīn,*" I practiced, shielding the sun with my hand over my eyes, trying to make eye contact with her.

With a hand on her hip, the tone in her voice was not at all friendly. Even in Mandarin, I knew I was not welcome.

*Christmas—Durban, South Africa. I'm seven.*

*Daddy's parents, my grandparents, had flown out to spend the holidays with us and be there for the birth of my sister. I was worried Santa might have trouble finding me, but Mommy and Daddy assured me he would know where I was.*

*Grandma, a professor at Duke University, was the only girl in the political science department. She wrote three books used at the State House. And she didn't even start formal schooling until she was in the sixth grade. And at twenty-one she was ready to graduate with a PhD,* but they made her wait a year for her diploma because she wasn't a boy. She was smart, like really smart.

Christmas Eve, she and I sat on the balcony discussing Santa's arrival. She looked me in the eye and said, "You know there is NO Santa Claus. He's made up—a fairy tale."

I shook my head. That couldn't be! How could such a smart woman say something so crazy? I couldn't believe I was being told such a thing! And by my grandmother.

I ran to my room crying.

It would be years later when we learned she was in the beginning stages of Alzheimer's. Duke asked her to retire early because she forgot she had a class, a test, or what she was teaching on any given day.

I put the puppy down and headed back across the street, wanting to believe she was going to be okay, tied to that fence. The shopkeeper's tone and disapproval made me more determined to keep showing up for this unloved pup.

# 37

"You have everything you need to cut the opening sequence."

Max was running; he had no time for me.

*Alone again.*

"Max, how was your day? What happened on the set?"

"So busy. So much to do. Gotta go. See you tomorrow," he said as he closed the door.

*So horribly alone.*

# 38

TODAY'S THE DAY.

*My first scene.*

*My first edit.*

The scene: a puppet play for children.

I pulled a wide shot of the puppet stage, its backdrop crafted from yellowed parchment paper. Then I selected a shot as the camera panned across it: detailed drawings of tall mountains among clouds with a house on a hill and a castle by the sea. The two sets would tell the story.

I then chose takes of shadow puppets: the sun and the moon.

Then takes of the girl shadow puppet and of the boy shadow puppet.

Then of them dancing together—the big dance.

Then there were the reverse shots of the children in tiny chairs enjoying the show.

I watched them interact with the play and picked takes where they looked happy, even though I had no idea what they were saying.

My script was in English, but the film was shot in Mandarin.

As much as I needed Max, this was a great opportunity for him to work on a set.

Besides, I had cut Spanish commercials, substituted a Spanish line for an English one.

I looked at the script notes and matched it to the take.

It was a five-minute scene broken down into many different takes. I watched the puppeteer's delivery, but had no idea what he was saying or how it matched the English script.

I played a few more takes.

Listened.

Looked for clues.

Cues.

And things that would help me know where I was in the script.

I played them again but had no idea whether the puppeteer was talking about the sun or the moon or the boy or the girl.

I chose another part of the scene, letting those takes roll, studying each one.

Here the delivery was different.

I could hear he said different things in each take and his actions were different, but I had no clue which take to choose, because I didn't know what he'd said.

My stomach tightened.

I began to feel scared—not being able to choose a take.

That had NEVER, EVER happened to me before.

I had always been able to choose a take—part of a take—a moment in a take—*something*.

Right then and there . . .

It occurred to me.

I'd had two years of Spanish in high school and I loved eating Mexican food, so converting a Taco Bell ad from English to Spanish was not the same as trying to translate Mandarin into English.

Shit! I didn't know a word of Mandarin until I met Vin, who had extended my vocabulary from "hello" to "thank you."

I had no idea what the character was saying and I was supposed to make choices.

Make an edit.

Cut a whole scene together.

*I'm out of my fucking mind to think I can do this.*

My body went numb.

My heart began to race.

I froze.

This wasn't what I signed up for.

What did I get myself into?

And this was . . . just the first scene. I had to cut ninety minutes of this film.

Every time Robert had pitched the project to me, he promised, "You can do this with your eyes closed, Lisa. Everyone knows the Cinderella story. It's just pretty pictures and iconic images." Yeah, well . . . I closed my eyes, but nothing came.

*What was I thinking?*

*Left in the middle of nowhere on my own, unable to understand anything.*

My breathing grew shallow.

I wanted to jump out of my skin.

My body wanted to flee.

This was a huge mistake.

I grabbed my coat from the back of my chair and ran down the staircase, taking each step with the anxiousness of needing to get as far away as I could. I ran through the empty parking lot and across the street, just missing a tuk-tuk.

My furry friend was still there, tied to the impenetrable fence.

I ran over, sat down, and put her in my lap.

I closed my eyes as I held her in my arms.

My heart was racing, but holding her calmed me. Eventually my breath began to sync with her breath, and we became one.

"Thank you for being here," I whispered as I felt myself settle back into my body.

When I opened my eyes, she looked up at me.

"I'm Lisa," I said, introducing myself. And you are . . ." I stared into her charcoal eyes, which stared into mine with wonder, took a deep breath in, and said, "Cinderella. You are Cinderella."

I began to laugh; she licked my face. The cold wind blew, covering us in red dirt. Dirt stuck deep down into my sunscreen, into the roots of my hair.

I looked over at the owner. Feeling dirty, I could feel the owner's eyes on us. She'd been pretending to be stocking her shelves and taking inventory, but I saw her watching me.

I was watching her watching me, with my new best friend, Cinderella.

# 39

THE NEXT DAY MAX STAYED BEHIND AND TRANSLATED THE FIRST scene for me.

When I saw it start to come together, I leaned over and said, "I made a new friend yesterday. Want to meet her?"

"Sure," Max said, not taking his eyes off the monitor.

It was late in the afternoon and the little stall was busy with two people shopping. A teenage girl bought a package of noodles while the second customer, a middle-aged woman, conversed with the shopkeeper.

"There she is, Max."

I ran toward her and took my seat in the dirt. Cinderella jumped in my lap and began kissing my face. Max knelt beside me and reached over to pet her.

"She's cute," he said while he petted her head softly.

"I've named her Cinderella."

"Cinderella," he said as he looked into her eyes.

The shopkeeper stopped and stared at us. Max had his back to her.

"Would you talk to her for me?" I asked in a whisper.

Max looked over his shoulder, stood up, walked over to the counter, and began speaking with her. He had such a nice way about him, all the older women loved him. He was handsome and charming and sweet. At least in English; I'm assuming he was that way in Mandarin, too. She didn't smile at him as she handed him a green glass bottle of liquid. I held on to Cinderella and watched, trying to figure out what was being said.

He handed her some money, took a sip from his bottle, nodded, and said, "*Shay shay.*"

It felt good to have Max with me again. To explain the world and other people for me.

"She said the puppy is for protection," he said.

"Yeah, she kept me away," I said, holding Cinderella as she kissed my face.

Max reached down and patted Cinderella on the head again. "I see why you like her." He took a seat next to me.

Cinderella stepped over and lay down in Max's lap with her head on his thigh.

"Some guard dog," Max whispered as he finished his drink, and we soaked up the sun until it was time to go back to work.

AND SO THE STORY BEGINS . . .

AGAIN!

# 40

MAX AND I SETTLED INTO A ROUTINE. WE'D HAVE BREAKFAST together each morning. Afterward, he'd translate the scene I needed to edit and then be off to the set, leaving me on my own.

Rain beat against my window while I sorted the morning's dailies.

The scene: Mei Mei is left to clean while Stepmother and Stepsister go into town.

Mei Mei, covered in soot, scrubs the outside cook area.

I studied Mei Mei's expressions in each close-up and chose the ones I felt conveyed the most despair—her shoulders slumped, her lower lip jutting out, her brow furrowed—and began to build my select reel.

I chose another shot where she cried, tears traveling through her soot-covered cheeks, to see how that played in the scene.

The next setup was from Mei Mei's point of view.

A medium shot of Stepmother and Stepsister looking down at Mei Mei from the road.

Stepmother's gestures look harsh and scolding as she looks down upon Mei Mei.

It's followed by a wide shot as she watches Stepmother and Stepsister walk away.

Their figures become smaller and smaller as they leave Mei Mei behind.

I was deciding which take to choose when I heard a loud bang on the door.

"It's Fred Simon!" yelled a voice in a Scottish accent from the other side.

"Hang on." I jumped out of my chair, excited someone had arrived who spoke English.

We could have a cup of tea together!

*A new friend!*

*Too bad I don't have any biscuits or scones.*

I opened the door and there, standing before me, was a pudgy man with red cheeks and red hair, not much taller than myself, drenched from the rain, carrying a well-worn brown leather satchel. He stepped on my foot as he pushed his way in.

"Would you like to come in?" I asked, taken aback by his lack of manners.

"I need to see the dailies!" he demanded.

Robert had mentioned one of the producers was coming to town, but hadn't said when. He also said under NO circumstances was I to show the dailies to ANYONE without him being present.

"Would you like a cup of tea?" I asked.

"No. I want to see the dailies."

"I'm afraid I've been asked not to show them to anyone unless Robert's here to show you himself."

My heart pounded. Taken aback by his rude behavior, I walked over and stood in front of the monitors, blocking his view.

"I'm not *anyone*. I am the producer of this movie and I demand to see them. NOW!" he roared.

He threw his water-soaked satchel on the sofa and followed it with a loud grunt.

*There goes my tea party.*

My body began to grow numb, my breathing shallow.

There is ALWAYS at least one producer on every movie that needs to scare the shit out of everyone . . . and he had just arrived to my edit bay.

Fred huffed and puffed as he paced back and forth, screeching into his mobile, "I'm here in Yunnan. The editor won't let me look at the dailies. Can someone get Robert on the phone?"

He finally took a seat on the sofa and began going through his satchel.

I sat down in my chair and began counting breaths, trying to change the energy in my room.

"Are you hungry?" I asked, trying my hand at being charming, but he immediately waved the question away.

"I need to see what's already been shot before I go to the set."

My phone rang.

"I guess you've heard Fred's here."

"I heard. I've got bigger problems. Chinese officials are on the set right now and complaining that our costumes are 'too Tibetan.' Whatever that means. There's talk of shutting us down until we change them. It's not how I wanted to do this but go ahead and show Fred what we've shot so far. I've gotta go." *Click.*

I spun around in my chair and waited while Fred finished his call.

"We have the go-ahead from Robert to look at the dailies."

"It's about time," he said smugly.

I started with shots of the children, hoping that would take the crankiness out of Fred. Their lovable faces, tiny hands with little fingers, dressed in such exquisite costumes, would surely make him smile.

*I* smiled, and I had already seen the film several times, but Fred was determined to hold tight to his ill-humored mood.

After I had shown him all the puppet play, we watched exterior village scenes, eventually showing him the scenes of Mei Mei covered from head to toe in soot.

She looked like I felt.

# 41

"HE MISSES YOU, TOO, BUT HE'S SETTLED INTO A ROUTINE HERE.
What do you miss besides Ron Howard?"

"Pizza . . . The crew food is minimal, and by that I mean cabbage with a few minute pieces of pork, white rice, and eggplant. I hate eggplant."

Mavis laughed. "Ron's definitely dining better than you on my leftovers. I was taken to Musso and Frank last night. Their rib eye is the best."

Mavis told me about her date. An old college boyfriend found her on Facebook and the spark was brighter than before. They'd met as fearless reporters for the school paper, *The Gator.* He had his own column covering the happenings on campus, she uncovering the latest school scandals.

"It's really nice having someone around, taking care of me. I'd forgotten how wonderful it is to be with the right person. People are there to take care of you, too, just like I'm taking care of Ron. You just need to relax and settle in."

"Let me look at him again. Please."

She moved her phone and I caught a close-up of Ron's button nose and a glimpse of his paw landing on a pile of dirty laundry next to an overflowing ashtray.

Mavis and I were two peas in a pod, having spent our younger years working hard in our careers—no time for marriage and relationships. At our age, children typically brought people together. Sugar Ray and Ron Howard brought us together.

After Mavis ended our call with a shot of her dirty clothes, I went back to work.

This morning's scene: Mei Mei's mother shows her the magic slippers she will one day wear to the dance. Black velvet with a large goldfish embroidered on each slipper, in the most vibrant shades of orange and yellow, trimmed in semiprecious stones and gold threads. They were beautiful.

With the goldfish symbolizing wealth and abundance, I wanted a pair.

I worked the scene, cutting different versions—from close-up to wide—from wide to close-up.

After editing the scene every which way I could think of, I needed a break.

Things were quiet around the hotel with everyone on set. I poked my head in the door of the production office and caught Sunny's eye.

"Got a few minutes?" I asked.

She nodded.

"I thought you might want to meet my new friend."

"You made a friend?" She flashed the biggest grin.

"Come. I'll introduce you."

As soon as she saw me, Cinderella jumped up on her hind legs and danced, pulling the fence as far as the short rope would allow her.

"Here she is. Cinderella." I squatted beside her before she jumped in my lap.

"Cinderella?"

I nodded.

"Oooh . . . I love her name. And she's so cute!" Sunny beamed as Cinderella jumped into her lap. "You have a dog, Lisa?"

"I do."

"You must miss him?" Sunny asked.

"I do, terribly."

"I can tell. The way you love this dog."

The sun disappeared behind the dark, ominous clouds, making it cold. The shopkeeper began packing up her goods. A big downpour was headed our way.

"We have to go. I hate leaving you here in the rain, Cinderella."

"I do, too," Sunny said with a frown on her face.


Eva was where we had left her, at her desk with her headset on. She looked up as Sunny and I giggled, soaked from the rain. She waved me over while she sorted through a pile of paper on her desk until she found a white envelope with my name on it: my per diem. She handed it to me while she spoke Mandarin into her headset. I tucked the envelope into my jacket pocket and headed back upstairs. It felt good to be flush again.

I watched the rain pour down my window as I went back to work, pulling selects of Mei Mei finding out her mother and sibling died in childbirth.

*When I was seven and living in Johannesburg, South Africa, my mommy got pregnant. Everyone was so excited.*

*I wanted a little sister.*

*I got a sister, but she was premature—weighing only three pounds.*

*My mommy lost so much blood they didn't think she would live.*

*My three-pound sister came home from the hospital five weeks before my mommy did.*

*I missed my mommy.*

# 42

MY LAST NIGHT IN NUODENG, I TOSSED AND TURNED IN BED.
It had been five long weeks. I was just beginning to get into a
rhythm and now we were packing up and moving to the next
location.

After breakfast, Max broke down our workstation while I
packed. Vin made the trek up and down the three flights of
stairs, carrying monitors, machines, and drives, followed by my
two seventy-pound suitcases. I was ready to leave this dusty little
village, but my heart ached for my furry little friend across the
street.

"I'll be right back."

I threw my backpack on the passenger seat and ran through
the parking lot, across the street, passing the shopkeeper—I
held Cinderella's sweet little face in my hands and looked deep
into her charcoal-black eyes.

"Thank you for being my friend. You were here when I really
needed one."

I didn't want to leave her *here*, tied to this fence.

I finally gave in to my sadness. Unable to hold it back any
longer, I wept into Cinderella's fur, hoping no one would hear
my heart breaking, her little body muffling my cry.

She licked my tears as fast as they streamed down my face.

I felt a hand on my shoulder and looked up.

It was Max. We'd been together for only a little over a month now and I felt like he was my family—my person. Poor guy. I never even asked how old he was. Twenty-two maybe? His first film. First time on the set. First time in mainland China, too. He could have been my son, but he felt like a younger brother.

My assistants in LA were so immature compared to him. Max radiated kindness. I could tell he wanted to please me, take care of me. But I never thought about who I was to him. Some old-maid editor from Hollywood, probably. Was I cool? Probably not with all my crying. But he was cool. Hell, he spoke four languages. Five if you count computer, which was a foreign language to me. I only knew how to power on and power off in that language.

"You okay?"

All I could do was shake my head.

"You don't want to leave her."

I shook my head and sniveled as I tried to catch my breath.

"She'll be okay." Max rubbed his hand under Cinderella's jaw all the way down the front of her light brown chest.

"I won't be, though."

Steeling myself, I ran back across the street and jumped into the front seat of our parked van. Max walked over to talk with Vin, who was smoking his cigarette. While rummaging for another package of tissues in my backpack on the floor, I heard a knock on my window and rolled it down.

"What's going on?" Robert asked.

"I can't believe that little dog's destiny is to be chained to a fence. I just don't understand how they can treat a dog that way."

Robert looked at his watch and then looked at me. "Go get her and bring her along. We'll find her a home."

"Really?"

"Yes. Go get her. We'll find her a home."

I sat there, bewildered.

"Hurry!"

"You sure?"

He nodded a firm yes and walked toward his van.

I jumped out of my seat and I yelled, "Come on, Max!"

"Where are we going?" Max asked.

"To get Cinderella!"

We dodged Robert's van as it pulled out of the parking lot before we crossed the street. Cinderella squealed as she pulled away from the fence when she saw us. I sat down and held her tight, whispering in her ear, "You're coming with us."

While Max spoke, the shopkeeper's blank gaze darkened and her eyes grew stern as she listened to his words.

*What did he just tell her? That I was difficult to work with and if I didn't get the dog, I would be the bitch?*

She looked over at me.

*Was she thinking I was some spoiled American?*

*I was.*

I pulled out fifty yuan from my per diem envelope.

She looked at me in a way she hadn't before.

"You can take her." Max smiled at me while he untied her rope.

"*Shay shay*," I said as I placed the money in the palm of her hand.

We ran back across the street, Max looking at Cinderella— he was just as excited to have our new crew member as I was.

I hopped in the van, fastened my seat belt, held Cinderella close, and whispered, "Hold on tight. Vin's driving." Before we drove to the edge of town, Cinderella threw up all over me. Not once, not twice, but three times.

Wouldn't you know it?

Cinderella had motion sickness and we had an eight-hour drive ahead of us.

# 43

I was never one to play with dolls, so when I turned four, my grand-parents gave me a fancy baby carriage for my birthday, in hopes that this might change things. It was white with big wheels and a royal-blue bonnet that fanned up and down to shade the baby doll from the sun. It came complete with a waterproof mattress that lined the bottom of the carriage for accidents, and a flannel blanket to keep the doll warm. Still showing no interest in dolls, I loaded up the carriage with my treasured stuffed animal collection and took them for a walk around the neighborhood.

What I really wanted was a dog, but my mother was allergic, so I was given more nontraditional pets. Leonard Warmfeet was my first pet, a neon yellow and green parakeet who was allowed to fly around our house and was quite the whistler. "Winchester Cathedral" was his favorite tune. One day I left the front door open, Leonard flew out, and I never saw him again.

Harold Browder was my next pet. He was a guinea pig who looked like my father's friend—hence his name. Harold lived in a cardboard box at the foot of my bed. One day, he caught my cold and died.

Then I got Thumper, my house-trained rabbit. He loved going for walks on a leash in a clover field on the sheep farm where we lived. Thumper was a great pal until we moved to Africa, and I couldn't take him with me. Dad said he went to live in a new home on a new farm.

On Christmas morning when I was eight, I got the second-best gift a kid could get for Christmas: an apple-green Schwinn three-speed bicycle with hand brakes, a groovy banana seat with green and purple flowers, and a white basket that hung from the monkey handlebars to carry my books home from school.

After showing it off around the block, I ran back inside, out of breath. Mommy had been crying. I gave her a big hug. She had on her lime-green cashmere cardigan. I loved it when she wore that sweater. I felt like I was wrapped up by a big momma bear. All safe and warm. Nothing could hurt me there.

Daddy finished cleaning up the kitchen, reached for a dish towel, dried his hands, and then threw it over his shoulder. Still in his red plaid robe and pj's, he turned off the Christmas music and sat down in his over-stuffed olive club chair.

"Your mother and I have something we want to talk to you about."

He looked straight at me and then over at Mommy, who was now sitting on the floor, crying.

I sat cross-legged, like we did at story time, back straight. Mommy reached for my hand.

"Your mother and I are getting a divorce," Daddy announced like he was going to the grocery store. "And we have decided that we are not going to separate you and your sister—that you will make the decision for the two of you as to who you'll both live with."

He ushered me to the stairs. "Go up to your room and think about it."

Daddy handed me a couple pieces of paper with a No. 2 pencil. "If it's easier for you to write it down, that's fine, too, honey."

I climbed the staircase to the second floor, one step at a time, holding on to the cold metal railing, staring at the blurred avocado-green shag carpet through my tears as I took each step—not wanting to make it to the top, not wanting to get to my room. I passed my sister's room, where she was asleep in her crib, the Snoopy music box on her dresser playing the last notes of "Fly Me to the Moon."

I climbed on top of my bed, my legs dangling over the side, and I looked at my Nancy Drew collection in the bookcase of the headboard. Each book lined up in numerical order—just the way I liked it. Christmas with The Chipmunks lay on the turntable of my yellow plastic record player, leftover from a Christmas Eve of nonstop dancing. Alvin. Theodore. Simon. I loved singing along with them.

With the No. 2 pencil in my hand, and the two pieces of paper, I sat and I waited while I stared around my room. My watery eyes landed on top of my bookcase—home to my stuffed animal family. They had always been there for me. There were the three bears—Mama Bear, Papa Bear, and Baby Bear—Lulu, the sandy-brown cocker spaniel that Gran bought me in Miami; and Teddy, the bear Aunt Babsie gave me the day I was born.

I thought of what Daddy's mommy, Grandma Cheek, told me just a month earlier in her bedroom. She was standing in front of her big double dresser drawers, a large round mirror sitting on top of it. Brushing her over-dyed dark brown hair, she caught my eye in the mirror while I was sitting on her four-poster bed.

"If your parents ever get a divorce, YOU choose to live with YOUR father," she instructed while she continued to brush her hair.

I remembered hearing those words and they frightened me.

I picked up the paper and pencil and wrote the note I knew I needed to write—one to Daddy and one to Mommy: "I love you very much, Mommy, but I think we need to live with Daddy. I am so, so sorry."

I folded up each piece of paper and slipped them both between the sliver of light under the door.

他妈的圣诞快乐

TĀ MĀ DE SHÈNGDÀN KUÀILÈ...

MERRY FUCKING CHRISTMAS

# 44

The next Christmas, the house was decorated, presents wrapped under the tree, Daddy still in his red plaid robe and pj's.

We unwrapped our gifts. All things I needed, clothes and notebooks for school.

Nothing memorable like a bike or a divorce.

Daddy said he'd forgotten something. He left the room and came up from the basement with a big cardboard box that had holes in it. He placed it on the floor in front of me. There was scratching coming from inside the box.

"Well, aren't you going to open it?" he asked.

The top flaps were folded loosely together, so I lifted them up, and out popped a black-and-white puppy on her hind legs.

A real live puppy.

Not a stuffed animal like I had received every birthday and Christmas before, but a living, breathing, honest-to-goodness pup. I picked her up and held her tight. Her hind legs dragged along the side of my body.

She sneezed. She sneezed again.

I sobbed—sobbed so hard.

"Why are you crying, honey?"

"I'm so happy," I wailed.

Daddy laughed while I did my best to hold on to my wiggly pup.

"She's really mine?" I double-checked, looking up at Daddy again, not really believing.

"She is."

Her ears were long, black, curved, and curly. Her body was white with black patches on it. She had a runny black nose, black eyes, and four little black and white puffy paws. She was better than anything I had ever dreamed of. And she was a girl.

I looked into those big black eyes. "We're going to be best friends," I assured her.

She sneezed again.

"What kind of a dog do you think she is?" I asked as her little teeth gnawed on one hand and my other hand rubbed her tummy.

"Heinz 57. A mutt. But the man I got her from thinks she's a poodle with some cocker spaniel."

I ran my fingers through her curly hair. It was soft and silky. She didn't sit still.

She sneezed.

"So, what are you going to name her?" Daddy asked.

"Sneezy. After one of the seven dwarfs."

She sneezed again.

Warm liquid sprayed my hand. I opened my eyes and looked down at Cinderella. She had car sickness bad, poor girl.

# 45

WE PULLED INTO A PACKED PARKING LOT—CARS PULLING IN AND out, people pushing shopping carts overflowing with purchases.

Cinderella stirred in my lap, smacked her lips together, and looked up at me, thirsty and dehydrated. I poured water into the cap of my thermos, where she gratefully lapped it up.

WALMART SUPERCENTER in large white letters with red Chinese characters below.

I hadn't seen modern English since the airport, but I had heard of this megastore from Eva and Sunny, where once a week Vin made a run to pick up extravagances like paper products and snacks. I might never see another superstore in China again, so I ran through the list of essentials Cinderella and I needed and followed the guys to the entrance.

It looked like any other Walmart.

Sliding glass doors.

Rows of red plastic shopping carts.

A vast cavern of fluorescent lights with aisle upon aisle of merchandise.

I placed Cinderella in the child's seat of my shopping cart and followed Max and Vin. Vin had long legs and walked as if he were late for a very important appointment.

Women's clothes filled the entrance: black stretchy pants

followed by rows of bright-colored jeans ending with a short rack of dresses.

I understood the need for such a small section of dresses: the women worked hard here—they ran everything. And you can't wear a dress while hiking up a mountain carrying a hundred-pound bag of rice on your back.

I picked up two small white bowls for Cinderella and made my way toward the food department, where I hoped to find Max, pausing to stock up on tissues along the way.

A couple of aisles over was the instant noodle aisle—the busiest department in the store. People squatting, reaching, and talking on their mobiles while they scanned every variety. Maneuvering my cart in and around the crowd shopping for shrimp, beef, chicken, and spicy noodles was no easy feat. Cinderella's nose perked up as she sniffed all the spices while we made our way down the aisle.

A man with his back to us juggled another cup of noodles to the pile he held in his arms.

"Max, is that you?"

"There you are." His voice sounded relieved, his arms piled high with Styrofoam cups.

"Want to put those in our cart?" I offered, giggling. "Quite the circus act you have going on there."

He dropped his noodles into the cart and petted Cinderella.

"She still looks thirsty. Can I give her more water?"

"Sure."

"Do you need any more noodles before we leave this aisle?"

Max double-checked his noodle selection in the cart. "No, I'm good."

"Great! Can you help me find the pet department?"

He led the way through the aisle of electronics. Cell phone cases, chargers, headsets, and earphones filled the aisle until it dead-ended. Against the wall sat a couple of bags of dog and cat food, a few leashes and collars, and a couple of dog beds. Owning a pet in China was a luxury, so the pet department was sparse, and what was there was expensive. I had to be thrifty with my per diem. I wasn't paid much to begin with, and my per diem was the only money I would be able to get a hold of. And now there was Cinderella I needed to take care of—so just the necessities.

Some food.

A collar.

And a leash for now, along with her new food bowls. I would feed her people food when I could, stealing from my breakfasts, lunches, and dinners.

Max picked up a red collar and leash and handed it to me. "In China, red symbolizes good fortune."

He picked out dog food and then led the way to the check-out counter, placing his goods on the counter first. From his backpack he took out his shopping bag and loaded it with all his noodles. After he paid, he placed my purchases onto the counter.

The man at the cash register looked over at me as he held the red collar and then looked at Cinderella in the child's seat. He made a loud huffing sound, placed the collar next to the dog food, and then picked up the leash. Max ignored our clerk's attitude while he packed my shopping bag. After paying the bill, I was left with only five yuan until next per diem payday.

Back at the van, Vin was in his usual stance, leaning against the driver's door, smoking a cigarette, chatting loudly on his mobile. In a far-off unfamiliar land, some things were becoming more familiar to me.

# 46

IT WAS DARK BY THE TIME WE REACHED SHAXI.

Not a hotel in sight.

Instead, the crew would be staying in guesthouses scattered throughout the little village. Our guesthouse was on a street that didn't allow cars, so Vin pulled up as close as he could and unloaded our bags. Big, beautiful trees created a canopy over the street. Max used his flashlight from his phone so we could see.

I attached Cinderella's new collar and leash and wheeled my carry-on down the wide, cobbled dirt road. She pulled in all directions, unable to adjust to her new lead, so I picked her up and carried her the rest of the way.

It was quiet, except for the low murmur of our voices.

We arrived at a large house—a two-story, mustard-colored building. One bright light hung over the entrance, illuminating a ramp that led down both sides of the building where some of our film crew stood drinking beers and smoking cigarettes, relaxing from the long day of travel.

Once Max informed us this was our new home, Cinderella and I walked up the ramp, through an old, weathered wooden door, and into a large, open reception room. To the right stood a tall black lacquer bar stocked with Pepsi, Coke, two types of beer, and a couple of tall bottles of liquor with handmade labels. In front of the bar sat four well-worn brown wicker barstools.

To the left was a social area with a brown leather love seat and two chairs.

In the corner stood a tall, narrow bookcase stuffed with paperbacks, mostly in Mandarin, a few in English, French, and German.

A pretty young Asian woman, dressed in jeans and a bright red down vest, with shoulder-length, shiny black hair and bangs, entered through the glass French doors in the back. She and Max spoke while Cinderella and I waited for instructions. I peered out back at an enclosed garden with lighted walkways lined with small wicker tables and chairs. A few more crew members filled the garden, talking and texting on their mobiles. To the back of the garden was a large, open staircase that led to the second story.

Finally free from her leash, Cinderella wandered around, taking in all the new smells while men moved bags and equipment upstairs. I looked up at the sky and saw stars, so many stars that night.

It was cold and it felt good to be outside after sitting in a car most of the day.

Standing still.

Breathing in fresh air.

Taking in my new surroundings.

"So it's you and me and the entire camera crew in this one guesthouse. You have the only room with a private bathroom," Max said.

"Really?"

I popped my head into the room entranceway, where on the

immediate left was a bathroom with a spacious shower and a Western toilet.

"Wang Lee has his own room across from you, but no bathroom. The rest of us will be sharing the community bathroom, which is right next to you."

Cinderella wandered in with Vin right behind her, bringing in my big bags. I was ready to get cleaned up and I smiled.

*My new home for the next six weeks.*

# 47

THE ROOM ITSELF WAS COMPACT: A BIG, QUEEN-SIZE BED WITH two tiny nightstands on each side, a reading lamp attached to the wall just above the headboard with a small digital clock on the table. At the end of the bed was enough room to walk between the bed and a tiny table with a kettle on it. Vin left a suitcase on a narrow desk for me to unpack. Across from the bathroom was a rod with one lone wire clothes hanger.

*Time for a shower.*

The water pressure was strong and the hot water helped release all the tension—the stiff muscles—from the day of travel, plus the vomit smell thanks to my new travel companion. I gave Cinderella a quick wash, too. With clean, fresh sheets, we were both asleep within seconds after I turned off the light.

# 48

My new roommates—the entire camera crew—had started their day.

Sounds of heavy objects being dragged through the courtyard, but I couldn't bear getting out of bed, so I turned over.

And there was Cinderella, lying next to my head, sleeping hard. Furthest thing from a watchdog.

I waited until my roommates left before I flipped on the kettle, picked up Cinderella, and took her out into the garden, where she would get used to her new morning routine.

*HIIIIISSSSS* went the kettle. I grabbed a cup of tea and took a seat on the patio.

Birds sang. The garden had that soft, early-morning, golden light that made everything magical.

For just a few moments I was in my own fairy tale. I had a little dog, Cinderella, whose destiny had been changed by her fairy godfather, Robert. He had waved his magic wand and declared she join the film crew where she'd traveled all day in her carriage, an old white van . . . arriving at the famous village known for the beautiful slippers they make . . . where a fabled ball was about to be filmed.

My dreaming was interrupted when Max bounced down the rickety wooden staircase channeling Gus Gus, Cinderella's enthusiastic tailor mouse. When he reached the bottom of the stairs, he stopped to pet Cinderella.

"Ready for breakfast?"

"You bet! I'm hungry."

*Please, not congee again.*

"It's just across the street."

We followed Max through the reception area—Cinderella surprisingly well adjusted to her lead now. We passed the stacks and stacks of anvil cases filled with our editing equipment.

"I'll set up everything after breakfast," Max said as he opened the weighty wooden door. "We have this entire reception area as our new office."

"I love it. So much natural light in here."

We walked outside, down the cement ramp, and onto the red dirt-cobbled road. Our tiny, carless street was charming and quaint—something I had been unable to see last night in the dark. So different from Nuodeng.

No tall buildings.

Not a tuk-tuk in sight.

Shaxi was a very old village.

Most of the buildings had been here a long time. Longer than the houses on the top of the mountain in Nuodeng.

Everything here felt ancient . . . so ancient it felt sacred.

We crossed the wide street, looking both ways out of habit. No need for that here. It was a "pedestrian only" road. At one end I spotted a woman sweeping the front porch. Dirt whirled around her like a tornado. I thought of Sugar Ray, ensconced in his dust cloud, and wondered how Ron was doing.

"I think this is it," Max said as we passed through a dark, weathered iron entranceway that felt so low it required us to duck under and step down through an archway. We made an immediate left turn that led into a corridor that spilled out into an exterior patio. Four large dining booths lined the two exterior walls, leaving the open area with four large tables and chairs. Sunny and Eva, already seated, waved us over.

"Good morning, Sunny . . . Eva," I said. Cinderella followed at my heels as we weaved in and around the chairs, Max and Eva conversing in Mandarin when Sunny screamed, "Cinderella! How did you get here?"

"She came in her carriage, of course." I giggled. "She wasn't about to miss the ball."

Sunny jumped out of her chair, ran over, and squatted down so Cinderella could jump into her lap.

"*Wǒ gǎndào hěn kāixīn!* That you came to join us in Shaxi!"

Cinderella's tail wagged back with glee.

Eva looked up at me.

"What happened?"

"I cried. Robert said, *Go get her—we'll find her a home.* So Max and I did."

Eva smiled, reached down, and petted her, too. "Cinderella. You got a happily ever after, that's for sure. Kitchen's over there." Eva pointed across the patio. "It's the usual."

*Bummer.*

Cinderella had a playmate in Sunny now while Max and I got breakfast. I'd forgotten to bring her new bowls, so I broke off a small piece of the sticky bun, scooped up some congee with it, and placed it on the floor in front of her. She gobbled it up, so I gave her a little more, this time with some egg on it. I was a little skittish not knowing what she had been fed in the past, and having been thrown up on all day yesterday, I was not going to feed her a whole lot of anything right away.

Eva asked if I needed to be on next week's visa run to Dali.

"Nope. I'm good."

"You sure?"

"The man I got my visa from said it was good for six months."

Cinderella licked the egg off of my fingers.

"Max, you need to renew your visa?"

"Yes."

"Then you'll go with Vin next Wednesday," Eva said as she got up from the table.

"Bye-bye, Cinderella. *Wǒ gǎndào hěn kāixīn*," Sunny said on her way out the door. "Oh, bye-bye, Lisa. Bye, Max."

"Wanna see where we're shooting the ball?" Max asked with the enthusiasm of a kid going to a water park.

"Yeah! That's why we're here!" I reached down and picked up Cinderella's lead.

"It's next to where we are staying."

Just beyond our guesthouse, our street opened onto a cobblestone square. In the middle of the square stood a giant tree. Naked. Not a leaf in sight.

Max held out both arms like he was a model for *The Price Is Right*, showing me the grand prize. "This is where the ball will be held. And over here," he continued, pointing to a three-story building with an ornate Chinese rooftop, "is the old Market Square Theatre. Chinese operas were performed here seven hundred years ago. At least that's what Vin told me."

I gazed into the open theater's second story—the high curved ceiling above the stage—studying its acoustic shaping, built to carry the sound to the crowd down below. Ocean waves, Chinese characters, and birds in flight painted among the ornate designs were carved in great detail for the audience to study while they listened to the stories presented from above.

A dragon and a phoenix arose from the center, signifying success and prosperity not only for the theater but for Shaxi.

Across from the Opera Theatre, Max pointed out a Buddhist temple painted a modest light brown; I wouldn't even have noticed it except the film crew had rented it out and were dressing it for the shoot.

We walked back to the guesthouse. Max began setting up our equipment while Cinderella and I took a seat on the stoop in front in the morning sunshine.

We watched an old man in a traditional navy-blue Mandarin jacket with a weathered face and a long white goatee saunter by, walking a goat sporting a matching goatee. I wondered where they were going looking so alike.

Across from the guesthouse, a woman opened wooden slatted doors, folding each panel as if she were closing a paper folding fan until I could see the entire contents of her shop.

It was a shoe store.

With shoes in every color.

Red.

Yellow.

Lavender.

Made in satin, velvet, and cotton.

Slippers with straps.

Open-toed slippers.

Slip-on slippers, like the ones you see in every Bruce Lee movie ever made.

The owner wore a black leather jacket with black jeans rolled up at the ankle, a simple pair of black cloth slippers—no socks—her long, straight black hair tied back in a knot at the nape of her neck. Chic. Just like you'd expect a designer to look. She sat behind an old black sewing machine with large gold Chinese characters along the top, her cheeks rosy from the chill in the air, smiling while she worked—something I hadn't seen in China, except when I was with Sunny. She was always smiling.

Our movie was about a girl and shoes—they called her shoe a slipper. And here I was in Shaxi, the most famous place in all of China known for their slippers. I wasn't about to travel all this way and not buy at least one pair.

"Max!" I yelled as I ran through the front door. "I need a new pair of shoes!"

# 49

I'D LIVED ALONE MY WHOLE ADULT LIFE, UNTIL RON HOWARD moved in, so sharing a house with thirteen men who didn't speak English was something I never even knew one could do. But here I was—in the middle of Shaxi, in a guesthouse just off the main square, living with a baker's dozen. There were never any formal introductions.

Maybe it was because I was the editor.

Maybe it was because I was a woman.

Maybe, just maybe, it was because no one spoke English, so no one introduced themselves.

I didn't know. But I chose to respect their boundaries, especially since we were living in the same house.

After dinner each night, my roommates relaxed in the garden, texting, talking on their mobiles, preparing for the next day. Max and I settled into our own routine in Shaxi, working much longer days—there was so much more footage to manage and cut.

The sun had set and the outside lights that hung against the guesthouse were on.

Wang Lee rolled out a mat and poured out a pile of white and black stones from a wooden box while his opponent took the seat across from him.

"Do you play?" Max asked as Wang Lee placed the first stone on the mat.

"What?"

"Go."

"No."

I watched Wang Lee's opponent, whom I'd never seen before, place his stone. "Who's that?"

"Zhang Wei, his gaffer. Wang Lee won't do a movie without him."

*Lighting is everything.*

As if on cue, the sky turned a deep black. Hundreds of stars filled the sky. The only time I'd ever seen close to this many stars at once was at a Hollywood premiere, and it wasn't anything close to this impressive.

A few of the cameramen brought in key lights to illuminate the table so the game would carry on.

I looked under my chair and gave the garden a quick scan, looking for Cinderella, but before I had a chance to search further, Wang Lee looked up at me and asked in Mandarin if I knew how to play. Max shook his head and said no. I smiled at Max, grateful he answered for me. Wang Lee had just added another stone to the board when, in my peripheral vision, I spotted Cinderella's tail in the bushes, by the staircase—dirt flying all around.

I ran over and grabbed her little body from behind—her snout hard at work in the dirt. She twisted her head around like a demon, growling, and bit down hard on my fingers.

I dropped her on the ground.

Blood gushed from two of my fingers. I ran across the garden back to my room.

*You little shit.*

My fingers throbbed as blood dripped from my hand. I washed my fingers under cold water, washing my blood down the drain.

"You okay?" Max popped his head in the bathroom.

"You can come in."

"What happened?"

"Cinderella's a biter! Please, tell everyone to be careful around her. I knew she must have been up to no good when I hadn't seen her for a while."

I pulled a tissue out of my pocket and wrapped it around my fingers.

"Do you need anything? Bandages?" Max's concern was comforting.

"I have some in my suitcase. I'll be okay."

Cinderella walked through the door.

Max scolded her, his face all scrunched up.

"I'm going to live if you are interested," I said, looking right into her little face. And then I looked at Max. "Thanks for checking on me. Can you find us the vet in the morning?"

"Sure."

As soon as Max left, Cinderella crawled under the bed.

I fluffed up my pillow and duvet, letting her know how comfortable it was going to be in the bed before I gave her a good long stare underneath on the floor. She didn't move, didn't even blink.

She knew what she had done was wrong.
You don't dig up the garden in the place you are staying.
And you certainly don't bite the hand that feeds you.
Everyone knows that.

# 50

I PEERED DOWN AT MY SHEETS—DRIED BLOOD STAINED MY pillowcase. Curled up next to me slept Cinderella, having found her way up in the middle of the night—the bite all forgotten on her end, snuggled up, as if nothing had happened.

Of course, she hadn't been humiliated in front of her roommates.

I rolled her over with a soft push.

"Come on, Cinderella—if I'm awake, then so are you."

I dropped her in the garden while I cleaned my wounds, got dressed, and walked into the office.

Max looked up from my computer screen, his eyes red from logging footage all hours of the day. "They shot a lot of footage yesterday," he said as he stretched his arms away from his torso.

I sighed. "They shoot a lot of footage every day."

# 51

ANOTHER DAY. ANOTHER SCENE.

Today: Mei Mei comes home to find Stepmother serving up her pet fish as the main dish to Stepsister's gentleman caller.

She watches them eat the flesh from the skeleton.

I close my eyes and want to cry.

*It was the middle of the night when Daddy woke me up.*

*He took me into their bedroom, where the bright overhead light blinded me.*

*A package was ripped open on the bed.*

*He picked up the tie from the tissue paper in the box.*

*"Is that yours, Daddy?"*

*His face turned that angry shade of red—a shade that I had seen before.*

*"You mother's having an affair."*

*At eight years old, I didn't know what that meant.*

*"Where is Mommy, Daddy?"*

*"She bought him a tie! It's that doctor. That doctor who delivered your sister. I knew it, and that's why she's leaving us."*

*I stood in my footed pajamas—frozen and scared.*

# 52

WITH CINDERELLA ASLEEP AT MY FEET AND MAX BEHIND ME at his desk, backing up the latest drive he received from the set, every day felt like Groundhog Day.

The footage changed, but the motions were the same.

Look at dailies.

Pull the shots.

Build a scene.

Send it to Robert.

Address his feedback.

Repeat.

This morning I watched take after take . . . after take . . . of trying to get a caged bird to fly out of its tiny door. Food had been hung from a limb just outside the cage to entice the bird, who had clearly dined before he came to the set.

So I waited: waiting for the one take when the bird would finally walk up to the door, spread his wings, leave the cage, and fly. Just then, the bird flew through the door, out the cage, and directly out of the shot, not across the front of the house like it was supposed to. My head hit the desk with exhaustion and exasperation.

"Max, I need a break. Wanna take a walk with us?"

Cinderella was up on her feet before Max could answer. "Yes."

I rolled my neck, first to the right, then to the left, and then my shoulders.

Cinderella jumped up on my legs so I could attach her lead.

Max set up a drive to load into my computer so there wouldn't be any downtime while we were out.

It was sunny but still cold outside. We passed the slipper lady—she was busy, her head down, guiding lavender silk through her sewing machine, making another pair of shoes. We passed Robert's guesthouse, where we spotted the woman who was always out front sweeping the porch with a passion. *He must have the cleanest guesthouse in Shaxi.* Such pride she took, cleaning the dirty porch each day. She must be the proprietor.

At the end of the square on the corner sat a small, one-story building where the windows had shutters closed tight since we'd arrived, but today they were open—wide open. A chalkboard stood out front with the word CAPPUCCINO written in large, bold letters. I stopped. Rubbed my eyes. Blinked several times, and read it again.

"Max, do you see this?" I asked, pointing to the easel.

"Cappuccino?"

"You see it, too?"

"I see it!"

"They have coffee with milk here, in this building, in Shaxi?"

"Let me ask."

He returned with a huge smile on his face.

"They have cappuccinos here!"

Being the only people in the small establishment, we took a table by a large picture window that overlooked the tiny square where the ball would be shot. Our waiter arrived. I motioned to Cinderella and asked in English, "Is it okay to bring her inside?"

Max translated—the man smiled and nodded.

*A place that served cappuccinos AND let dogs inside. I must be dreaming!*

While Max ordered, I closed my eyes and thought about the last time I had a coffee. It was over seven weeks ago, in a land far, far away. With Ron Howard. I missed my sweet boy. The way he sat so tall, how he loved eating a Fuji apple, and that I knew he was afraid of German shepherds. I looked at my bandaged fingers and then over at Cinderella. I didn't know anything about this one—except she didn't like to travel and got scared being approached from behind. I really missed my boy, Ron.

"I asked about the vet. He only comes one day a month and was just here."

"Well, I don't have lockjaw and I'm still breathing. So I guess she's okay."

The smell of coffee filled the air with our barista balancing two white cups and saucers on a tray. He placed one in front of me.

"It looks like the real thing," I said as I examined the color while breathing in the flavor. That sweet, caramel, nutty fragrance. The familiar smell of home. The deep brown color with just the right amount of dense white swirl on the top that could be nothing other than cow's milk, something I hadn't seen since we'd been on the mainland.

I took a long, slow sip and was in heaven.

Heaven had come to Shaxi.

I took another sip. I was warm now, and it brought me a comfort from home that made everything all right. I had forgotten such a luxury even existed. I wasn't tired anymore. My fingers didn't hurt.

I raised my right hand with two fingers outstretched, motioning for our barista to bring us two more.

# 53

SLEEPING THE DAY AWAY WAS NOT AN OPTION. AS WITH every day, there was too much work to be done. I waited until I heard the last pair of feet cross the office floor followed by the slam of the front door. Cinderella had become accustomed to sleeping through the morning rush hour. I listened to her breathe and thought of Ron—how he looked at me with his chocolate wafer eyes lined in black, the way Elizabeth Taylor wore her eyeliner—thick and pronounced. It was every girl's dream to wake up with her eyes made up like that.

I opened the door just in time to see the night sky turn light.

The smell of fresh hay in the air.

A rooster crowing in the distance.

Against the back wall, the forest-green bushes glistened from the overnight moisture. Cinderella started her morning search, sniffing for the perfect spot to take care of business. She had learned to do things on her own, so I started to take care of my own morning business, giving my face a good scrub, followed up with my sunscreen ritual—a must in my beauty regime, only to sit in a dark room all day.

I hit the Skype button.

"Hang on." Mavis answered her phone with a close-up of her

nostrils that blurred down to a pile of newspapers and eventually panned over to the bed where Ron was, stretched out among all the blankets and pillows, sound asleep. He was such a bed hound like me. Sugar Ray's head snuggled up to Ron's back legs, his tiny tongue hanging below his lips.

"What's new there?" Mavis asked.

"Another day—another scene to cut." I looked at the bags under my eyes in the tiny square off to the side of my screen. "Oh yeah," I added, shaking my head in disbelief. "And today is my birthday."

I leaned in closer, squinting to see if I had any visible gray hairs.

"Happy birthday! That's exciting!" she said, as she framed the camera upside down on her face. "How are you celebrating?"

"I wanted to sleep through it. I guess I'm celebrating right now, with you guys." I looked at Ron's furry little face. His whiskers were long and fox-like. I wanted to reach through the screen, grab him, and bring him back to Shaxi for the day.

"Don't they celebrate birthdays there?" Mavis asked, while she inhaled a freshly lit cigarette.

"I'm not telling anyone it's my birthday. I aged out of my last job. Can't have that happen in the middle of this job. In the middle of nowhere."

"I thought they love old people over there."

"The only old people I see around here are either alone, carrying a fifty-pound bag of rice up the side of Mount Everest, or. . . escorted by an ass."

"How's your new friend? Has she drawn any blood lately?" Mavis asked, as if she were covering the front-page story for the *National Enquirer* on an outbreak of vampires.

"No. And the vet situation sucks here."

And just like that . . . Cinderella promenaded in, jumped up on the bed, fluffed up her pillow to her liking, and sat down as if it were her throne.

Ron lifted his head off of the bed and tilted it toward the phone as if he recognized my voice.

"Hey, Ron." I reached for his tennis ball on the night table, holding it toward the screen. "Has he been playing ball?" I asked Mavis.

"I took him to the empty parking lot early Sunday morning and threw it around. He had such a good time. We all cheered him on while he chased each ball as if he were an outfielder at Dodger Stadium." She smiled as she petted his head. "He's such a star. Our own Roy Campanella."

She then filled me in on her romance. It was moving fast—as in he was moving out to LA and in with her. She'd lived with someone only once before and had sworn she'd never do it again, but she said, "It's all about the YOLO now."

"What's YOLO?"

"You. Only. Live. Once. It's time for us to go for our walk."

Ron and Sugar Ray heard the word "walk" and they both jumped off the bed.

"Happy birthday!" she yelled before the screen went black.

Yesterday's clothes were dumped on the floor; this week's per diem still sat in its envelope on the table. I'd been too busy to organize—to pick up. My vest rested on top of the pile. It needed to be hung up.

I looked over at the empty hanger in the closet.

# 54

Daddy grilled his favorites: hamburgers and hot dogs.

Mommy baked my favorite: vanilla cake with vanilla icing.

When Mommy walked in with all nine candles lit, she glanced over at her two powder-blue Samsonites, locked and tagged by the front door. Tears rolled down her face while she tried to smile as she sang "Happy Birthday." Daddy picked up the tune and sang it to the end.

I made a wish.

Mommy blew her nose while I blew out the candles.

I unwrapped my gifts—three Nancy Drew books I asked for.

Mommy disappeared upstairs while Daddy and I cleaned the kitchen.

We didn't talk.

I cleared the table.

He put away the leftovers.

He washed the dishes.

I dried them.

The next morning, the house was quiet. I walked down the stairs in my smiley pajamas. A ray of sunshine burst through a window, blinding me. For the last three steps, I held on to the black metal railing, squinting, as I stepped down into the living room. I walked past the big round coffee table that once belonged to my grandmother, then by the large console television where I watched Captain Kangaroo in the morning and *The Banana Splits* after school. Next to the television stood a bookcase filled with paperbacks by the front door, where the ray of sunshine ceased.

The suitcases had disappeared.

I stood in the empty space, my bare feet on top of the cold, black-tiled entranceway.

I looked at the closed coat-closet door, took five small steps across the icy tiled floor, and stood still in front of it. It was white with a gold doorknob. Parts of the shiny metal had been chipped away.

I took a big breath in, held it for a second, and then let it out before I reached for the cracked knob. It had a small round button in the center. I began to turn it to the right, ever so slowly, until the door popped as the clasp released, allowing the door to open wide.

I stood there.

Looking up.

In the middle of the closet where my mother's black-and-white herringbone overcoat hung now dangled an empty wire coat hanger.


I sobbed in my bed until I used up all the tissues. Once I caught my breath, I hung up the clothes on the floor and put on yesterday's ensemble. I opened the door, allowing Cinderella to walk down to the office with me, where she ran right over to Max, who was sitting at my desk loading footage.

"Good morning, Cinderella," he greeted as he reached down to pet her on the head.

"We're going for a cappuccino—maybe four," I said as I put on my sunglasses.

# 55

SHOE LADY WORKED AWAY ACROSS THE STREET.

Today's pair: black velvet.

"*Nǐ hǎo*," I said.

"*Nǐ hǎo*." She smiled, looking up from her sewing machine while she held her fabric down, completing her seam.

Our little street was deserted this morning. We passed Robert's two-story guesthouse with the stone slab for a bench out front. It sat vacant, and the proprietor, who was usually sweeping the entrance in the morning, had already come and gone. It still felt dirty, even though she probably already swept it today.

The magnificent ancient tree on the square stood strong as we crossed over the old, uneven paved courtyard to where the shutters had just been opened. The owner, who I now affectionately called "Joe," was placing his easel outside the front door.

Cinderella and I took our usual spot, the booth with a huge picture window of the square.

Joe held up his index finger. "One cappuccino?"

I smiled. *Now this is the way to celebrate my birthday.*

I gazed out on the square. Across it, tarps were draped into a small room. A twelve-foot, circular white paper accordion hung from the top of a tree next to the entrance. A young man dressed in blue jeans and a brown suede coat, donning a white paper garrison hat worn sideways, stood at the entrance of the makeshift tent. An old woman sat on a tiny stool next to him. An old man with a wispy white beard stood next to her. It moved with the slight breeze as he spoke to her. She looked up at him, squinting through the morning sun.

The smell of coffee grounds and a cappuccino slid onto my table, right under my nose. I inhaled, exhaled, and said, "*Shay shay.*"

Joe nodded.

I raised my hand, pointing to the activity across the way, and shrugged.

Joe responded in Chinese.

I shook my head, holding my palms up in question.

Joe stared off into the square, scratched his chin, and said, "Dead."

"Ah. Funeral, of course."

"Funeral." He stumbled as he tried to repeat what I said. Then he stood still for a second, not even breathing, as if he were paying his respects from afar. Then nodded at me, and at Cinderella before he left our table.

I sat alone with my thoughts. *Was it the old woman's husband and the young man's father who lay in the tent?* No one else came to pay their respects while I enjoyed my second cappuccino. It made me sad to think whoever lay in that tent didn't have many friends, but then I thought maybe he'd outlived them all and I wanted to cry.

*I wasn't allowed to cry when I was little. I wasn't allowed to talk about Mommy or cry about how much I missed her.*

*Before she left, she packed up all her things in big brown boxes and stored them in the basement.*

*After she left, I'd go down there.*

*To sit among the boxes.*

*To be with her.*

*And cry.*

*I would open one particular box. Inside was an old blue crystal perfume bottle with a silver extended atomizer pump.*

*I sprayed it.*

*It smelled like her.*

*It sparkled like she used to.*

*It felt magical every time I touched it, and it reminded me I would see her again.*

I wiped my nose as I watched the old lady begin to pack up her things.

The funeral was over.

I thought I better get back to finish cutting Mei Mei digging that grave scene before I had dug my own.

# 56

THE LOCATION WAS DESOLATE.

A single leafless tree, the land barren brown.

Giant, rocky mountains far off in the distance.

The naked tree provided nothing but a marker as Mei Mei dug her father's grave alone on an overcast day. She dug at the dirt with a round, shallow woven basket, using both hands to remove the dirt from the hole she dug around herself.

I scrolled through the wide shots, looking for the best composition of Stepmother and Stepsister standing up on a cliff, calling down to Mei Mei below.

Stepmother, dressed in her Sunday best for going into town, wore a huge sterling silver collar necklace that I coveted. I wondered where the costumer had purchased such a beautiful treasure. I had not seen any jewelry stores anywhere we had been so far, much less anything as beautiful as the pieces the women in the film wore, and I wondered if I could buy a few for myself when the shoot was over. If I were home today, that's exactly what I would be doing. Buying myself a piece of jewelry on my birthday, probably something in silver, too—at Tiffany's. I'd resorted to shopping on the film I was cutting, I was so desperate to shop. To experience pretty things again, feel something luxurious. To go to Barneys and buy something extravagant to wear. I was tired of wearing sweats. I wanted to wear a pretty floral dress and go to the ball like Mei Mei.

I loaded the reel of close-ups of Stepmother yelling at Mei Mei.

I looked for the one where Stepmother looked the meanest.

I found one where her lower jaw jutted out, her eyes squinted tight with a scowl, and her brows furrowed so deep they could hold a pencil.

Behind me, I heard the grinding of Max's chair against the tile floor as he moved away from his desk, followed by, "I'm going down to the set to pick up this morning's dailies. Need anything before I go?"

"Would you bring back lunch?"

My lower back ached. I stood up and stretched my waist, arching over to the right, reaching my left arm up and over my head, and held it while I counted to twenty, then repeated it on the other side. My right arm and shoulder felt tight and ached from nonstop working in the same position. The desk setup on the road was not ergonomically correct for any body type, leaving my whole right side, from the neck down to my fingers where I reached my trackball, strained. I wiggled my fingers and held the position longer on this side.

I squatted down with my arms out like a football player at practice and petted Cinderella under the chin. She rolled over, giving me her light brown tummy to rub while I rolled my neck around from side to side. Max and I did the best we could with the height of the chair to the table to the monitors, but there was only so much you could do when what you had was not adjustable. I stood up and stretched my arms away from my body, moving them in circles. My eyes needed a break, so I opened the front door and stood at the entrance.

The street was quiet today. I watched Shoe Lady sew yellow silk shoes. She worked with her neck down, guiding the fabric through her machine, and I wondered if she had neck issues, too. Two actors walked by dressed in costumes on their way to the set, deep in conversation. They were the king's advisors. His military confidant was bald, tall, and quite round, dressed in a red-and-blue-horizontal-striped suit with a white fur collar. Around his large tummy was a wide brown leather belt and he wore matching knee-high boots. The king's astrologer sported a pale green floor-length coat with a hat that looked like a lampshade, embellished with purple string dangling all around it, reminding me of a mop.

"*Nǐ hǎo.*" I waved.

They both looked at me and waved.

Shoe Lady looked up from her sewing machine and replied, "*Nǐ hǎo,*" with a smile.

Another way to start the scene came to me. I'd begin with a close-up of Mei Mei's dirty face as she wipes her forehead with her soiled hand, then cut to a medium shot, revealing her digging a grave.

I walked back over to my chair and began to cut the scene, ending on the wide shot with Stepmother yelling down at her. "You better finish digging your father's grave by the time we get back."

I watched the dailies again, choosing more pieces and adding them to my select rolls. Then I watched my select roll again, pulling pieces I'd missed the first time and using them in the next version I cut, seeing how the new pieces added to the scene.

Trimming.

Lengthening a shot.

Then I cut the exact same scene, this time as a wide shot.

Lastly, I cut another scene with Stepmother's line in the middle of the scene, framing Mei Mei's alone time at the beginning and the end, cutting different moments of Mei Mei alone in between.

Trying different takes.

Cutting shots in different ways.

Max interrupted my focus. "I found out where we can get one of those baskets for Cinderella. I thought we could take a walk there before dinner."

"Great. My eyes are tired and Mei Mei has dug enough for the day."

# 57

AS WE PASSED THROUGH THE SQUARE, THE FUNERAL HAD MOVED out and the production crew had moved in. Small trees and bushes dressed the front of each building while Wang Lee discussed lighting with his gaffer. The ball required three weeks of night shooting and they were starting tomorrow night.

In our Chinese version, Cinderella's slippers flew, so we stopped to watch while Jackie Chan's stunt crew began rehearsing. Wires hung from the rooftop of the opera house to the surrounding two-story buildings. Three strong men harnessed up the small stunt girl through a hook wrapped around her lower back.

They did a safety check, lifting her a few feet off the ground. Then they lifted her up among the trees and onto the rooftop, allowing her to safely leap from one rooftop to another—all done with the grace, style, and agility of Jackie Chan. When she finished her stunt, she did a double somersault from the rooftop, landed on her feet, and continued walking as if she were on her way to the market.

Max and I clapped with enthusiasm.

I threw my thumb and forefinger in my mouth and whistled, demanding an encore.

Max looked at me . . . but said nothing.

A few workers on the square stared at me.

We ducked under an archway that led to a tiny narrow alleyway between two-story homes that were locked up for the winter. The alley led to a dirt road that ran parallel to the main road. Between this road and the main road was a huge chain-link fence.

Max said they had a market here every Friday.

It was no Rose Bowl, but it was bigger than my local Starbucks.

We passed a woman with a weathered face carrying two large, heavy wooden buckets. One in each hand. She was strong and steady. I wondered what my life would have been like had I been born here. What would my buckets be filled with? Did she wonder about me?

Max stopped at a barnlike structure and knocked on an old wooden door. A weathered woman with a crooked nose wearing a cherry-red newsboy hat and matching down jacket greeted us. When Max explained why we were there, she opened her door wider, revealing a barn full of baskets. Towers of baskets that were two times taller than myself. More stacks than I could ever get through.

The sun was low in the sky, and with no electricity in the barn, our sales lady left the door open to catch the last of the natural light. Cinderella and I took a seat on the cold stone floor so we could look at the backpacks that the locals used to carry their shopping. They were rectangular, made from a wire frame to fit on a person's back, the basket woven in different-colored strands of plastic ribbon wrapped around the wire frame. *What a great bed for Cinderella to rest in while I worked!* There were so many color combinations to choose from. Max helped the woman pull a few apart from one of the teetering towers. We studied each one, eventually choosing a neon-pink and navy-blue basket. Max negotiated a price.

"A basket for my birthday!" I said to myself, unthinking, as I admired my beautiful new purchase among the dirt and hay on the floor.

"It's your birthday?" Max asked.

"Did I say that out loud?" The cat was out of the bag. I was now another year older.

"Happy birthday!" Max said as he held out his hand. "She wants ten yuan for the basket."

I placed Cinderella in her new home. Her body was long enough that if she sat on her back legs she could see out. I laced both arms through the side loops, hoisting her up on my back, and stood up.

Max smiled as he watched. "She likes it there. Let me take your photo."

It was getting dark as we returned to the square. It was quieter than before. Jackie Chan's people were still flying across the rooftops, but the production designer and his crew, along with the set dressers, had left. We stopped to watch the stunt people fly through the air. *Such a different job from editing*, I thought, as I watched them dance among the treetops.

What a birthday! Two cappuccinos, a shopping excursion, and a show. One might have thought I spent my birthday in Beverly Hills. *AND I could have bought more shoes . . .* I thought as I glanced at the shoe shop across the way while Max opened the front door to the guesthouse.

# 58

生日快乐
"Happy Birthday"

生日快乐
"Happy Birthday."

生日快乐
"Happy Birthday."

生日快乐

生日快乐

生日快乐

SO CHANTED OUR OFFICE, PACKED WITH CREW, MOST OF WHOM
I'd never seen before as we entered our guesthouse.

Max lifted Cinderella out of her new backpack and handed
her to Sunny while he stored my new purchase under my desk.
He placed a large paper crown adorned with jumbo red Chinese
characters on my head. Below them, in much smaller blue type,
read the words HAPPY BIRTHDAY. Super Mario, dressed in his
signature mustache, blue overalls, and red newsboy cap, adorned
the sides, making me feel quite hip in my new party hat.

The crew parted as Max and I moved through the crowded

room, revealing a table with an enormous cake. Pink, orange, and green roses edged the two-layered white icing extravagance—six skinny pink candles lit. Holding on to my paper crown, I made a wish and blew all the candles out. Everyone applauded, with Max announcing, "Now it's time for dinner. We have beer and a party planned."

Carrying Cinderella like a child on her hip, Sunny grinned. "Happy birthday!"

I reached over and hugged her, hugging Cinderella by proxy. "Let's put her in my room while we eat."

We walked through the crowd, passing the crew on their way to dinner. Once inside my room, I placed the new basket next to the bedside table, picked up a dirty T-shirt, and threw it in. Sunny stood inside the doorway, watching me.

"You can put her down now. I don't want her begging for food. She can join us later."

"Wanna Be Startin' Somethin'" boomed from the speakers. Max greeted me with a beer and a bowl. I took a seat on the sofa and dug into tonight's feast. White rice, green beans, and cabbage with a couple of pieces of pork the size of a shirt button. Max sat beside me.

"I let it slip an hour ago. How did you plan this so fast?" I asked as I took a swig of beer.

"We have our ways," he said with a sly smile. "We wanted to show you a good time being so far away from home."

"You have. Thank you." I smiled, a heart full of gratitude, as I looked around the room. A party filled with people eating and laughing. I hadn't seen anyone have this much fun since we'd been together.

After dinner, I walked into the courtyard. All my roommates were there—the crew talking, drinking, and laughing. I didn't know these men's names or their stories. If they were married or single. If they had children and grandchildren. But I did know tonight they wanted to party and the celebration was for me.

I opened the door, allowing Cinderella to finally attend my ball. She was ready to party just as "The Way You Make Me Feel" filled the courtyard. I love that song. I felt loved and I felt celebrated tonight.

So I danced.

Sunny ran over, skipped a circle around me, threw her arms up in the air as the song kicked in, and danced with me. Mei Lei, the beautiful costume designer, joined us. Around her neck, a gold skeleton key dangled from a chain, bouncing up and down to the beat of the music. She and Sunny moved their hips together in that Michael Jackson way, giggling as they did.

Soon the song changed to "Thriller," which brought the whole party out to the sunken garden. Everyone knew all the dance moves—each movement made with the exactness of Jackson himself. No one missed a beat. Not a limb out of place. It was a performance the icon himself would have been proud of.

On the other side of the porch, by Wang Lee's room, I watched him set up a couple of spotlights. When "Thriller" came to an end, the spotlights turned on . . .

Transforming the porch into a stage.

The steady drumbeat began.

Bass and guitars and then finally the organ.

The wooden shutter swung open from Wang Lee's bedroom window.

A hand with a white glove appeared.

His woolen flat cap tipped to the side of his head, covering his eyes while he waited for the lyrics to begin.

*She was more like a beauty queen from a movie scene.*

The guy seated next to me let out a howl.

"Billie Jean."

Someone whistled while Wang Lee walked out from behind the window, snapping his right fingers to the beat as he stepped toward us, shaking his hips back and forth, kicking his foot out in a way that only Michael Jackson did, gyrating his hips, leading to the ever-so-famous crotch-grabbing move.

He danced with style.

Each movement leading swiftly to the next.

I was mesmerized.

Here, in a tiny village thousands of years old in the middle of nowhere, Michael Jackson's music and dance was the language we all knew. It connected us in a way that no spoken word ever could or would.

# 59

"WHERE DID YOU FIND A CAKE?"

"Vin picked it up in Dali."

I scanned the room for Vin and found him leaning against the wall.

Our eyes met.

He raised his bottle of beer to me.

I placed my hand over my heart.

He smiled at me.

After cutting the cake, I arranged each piece around the table.

Wang Lee picked up a plate, smashing it into Max's face.

Max opened his eyes wide, looking shocked. Icing and cake hung from his nose.

*Is this a Chinese birthday tradition?*

Max smiled before he threw his plate at Wang Lee, hitting him in the ear.

Wang Lee laughed, picked up another piece of cake, and threw it at me.

Next thing I knew, there was cake flying everywhere.

It wasn't a Chinese tradition; it was my birthday.

Once all the cake was thrown, the party was over.

It was the best birthday *ever*.

# 60

No footsteps charging up and down the staircase.

I closed my eyes. Quiet—minus Cinderella's old man snores and my happy memories.

Last night's surprise party filled me. We ate, drank, and joyously danced the night away, closing out the party like five-year-olds on a playground. I'd thrown myself parties in the past, but I was too busy introducing people and making sure that my guests had a good time. I don't think *I* ever had a good time. Not like last night, where I was entertained. And certainly not one that ended in a food fight.

I rolled out of bed, fumbled my way over to my suitcase, and rummaged through it, pulling out the first pair of sweatpants I came across. A good packing tip: packing only one color allows one to get dressed in the dark and requires no thought.

"Time to go, Cinderella." I clapped my hands together.

All the outside lights were still on. A few mementos from last night's soiree remained.

Lone beer bottles left standing.

Smeared icing in the most random places: along the planter wall, the back of a chair, the bottom of the flag on a light. But a serious attempt had been made to clean up.

Max waved as he crossed the garden. "Morning."

"Morning. Where is everyone?"

"Asleep. They start night shooting tonight."

"Oh, right, I forgot. The ball begins."

Max walked through the office, sat down in my chair, and began to check the dailies he'd left loading overnight. There were crumbs of cake and smeared icing stuck to the window. I wiped it with the palm of my hand and smiled.

"You're all ready," Max said as he stood up from my chair.

"Sure." I slid comfortably into my seat, taking control.

# 61

When I was three, my father left the navy and moved us to Chapel Hill, North Carolina. We lived in a small white house owned by his parents—my grandparents—where my mother taught the third grade while my father dropped out of law school because there was too much reading for him and got his master's in political science instead.

After Daddy's last class for the day, he would pick me up from preschool and we would watch reruns of The Andy Griffith Show. Daddy looked just like Andy with his thick curly hair, and being from North Carolina, he not only spoke like him—he had his manners, too. I loved Opie. He loved his pa and the two of them looked out for each other, with Aunt Bee supplying the cooking. I'd felt akin to Opie ever since; that's why I named my dog Ron Howard. We were family.

Friday afternoons, the local channel aired an afternoon movie. Daddy loved movies. After my parents got a divorce, he used to take us to the drive-in for a double feature. He'd pop Jiffy Pop popcorn on the stove. I'd watch the tin foil grow and grow until the popcorn was ready. He'd slather it in butter and salt and throw it in a brown paper bag, fill the cooler full of sodas and beer, and pile us in the back of the station wagon with sleeping bags, stuffed animals, and pillows, where we'd fall asleep before the first movie even ended.

*Daddy took me to see* Mary Poppins *three times in one week. I loved that movie. I had a crush on Dick Van Dyke. That was a man who knew how to have fun—dancing with penguins, tea parties on the ceiling, and singing with animals. It would be decades later, when I was at a fundraiser for Best Friends Animal Rescue in Malibu, that I found myself standing next to Dick Van Dyke himself, outside in front of the porta-potties. It's there I got the chance to tell him how much joy he brought to my childhood. I still can't stop smiling when I think of him to this day.*

*I never planned to be an editor.*

*Daddy dropped me off at college my freshman year where he had enrolled me as a business major. "Don't come home until Thanksgiving,"* *he said. As soon as he left campus, I changed my major to communications. Let's just say he wasn't pleased when I communicated that.*

*I started out in local news running the teleprompter, then ran the on-set camera for* The Six O'Clock News *and* The News at Eleven— *that was until the sportscaster threw a chair at me. He'd run in a few seconds before the camera cut to him only to discover he was sitting in a chair without casters—making him appear much shorter than he already was. This was far from a lone incident. Daily outbursts were the norm.*

*In addition to the prima donnas that infiltrated this fiercely competitive market, it was a seriously intense twenty-two minutes and thirty seconds. I was constantly on the edge of throwing up, and that didn't include the content we aired every day. The only good thing about it was when* The Six O'Clock News *ended, there was no* looking back. We were all too busy getting ready for *The News at Eleven.*

Lucky for me, someone in the commercial department left to pursue their dreams, leaving their day job open—allowing me a chance to escape my nighttime gig. In those days, television station affiliates edited on tape. I didn't know anything about editing and they had only one editor, Robbie. Robbie was a big teddy bear of a guy. Long-haired hippie who grew up on one of the islands in Charleston. He'd let me hang out with him in my spare time and talk about his machines and how he edited "on the fly." He loved his job and there was something about it I thought I'd be good at, but Robbie wasn't going to be leaving anytime soon. Fate stepped in: a new TV station was signing on in town. I applied for their editing job.

They asked, "Can you edit?"

"No."

They said, "Great! We'll teach you."

So my next job was editing swear words and nudity and cutting commercial breaks into movies. During sweeps month when the Nielsen ratings were being taken, we would have Alfred Hitchcock Week, Clint Eastwood Week, and Meryl Streep Week.

I watched fifteen hundred movies in eighteen months. That was my film school.

# 62

BY MIDDAY, THE ROOMMATES STARTED TO SURFACE. ON occasion I would look through the glass door into the garden to give my eyes a break from the screen and spot one walking by wearing a towel around his neck, carrying his toiletries to the communal bathroom, or another carrying a pile of clothes on his way to the washing machine.

Cinderella had made the new basket her own. I placed it under my desk on its side, hoping she would crawl in and stay out of the way. Instead, she liked to sit on the top, allowing her a better look at everything going on around her. I wouldn't call her a guard dog, just a nosy dog.

More roommates gathered in the garden. A few on mobiles while several rested in chairs with their eyes closed. All the men looked relaxed, soaking up the warmth of the sun.

Wang Lee, humble as ever, set up a barber's chair in the center of the yard to cut his crew's hair. With his electric shaver, he groomed any volunteer. From my desk I watched as he clipped newspaper pages around the shoulders of his recruit and began to shave the right side of the head, then moved to the left side, saving the top for last. He smiled as he worked, chatting while the hair sprinkled from the razor's teeth onto the newspaper.

Occasionally, a slight breeze would catch a few hairs and blow them around the garden like dandelion seeds in a field, landing somewhere among the cobbled pavement.

It was a beautiful day from where I sat. The sun, that soft winter light. I didn't think I'd ever been to a barbershop before, and here one had come to me. Right in the garden of my guest-house, just outside my edit bay.

When Wang Lee finished one head, he'd remove the newspaper from their shoulders, shake it out, and make room for his next client.

Being so engrossed in the scene I was cutting, by the time I had a chance to look out again, the barber's chair was gone. The tranquility of the day had turned to a mad rush out the front door to set up for the first night shoot. Even Max couldn't wait to get to the set.

While everyone else went to the ball, Cinderella and I were left alone to cut the next scene: Stepmother teaching Stepsister to dance. I cut late into the night, working until my neck and shoulders ached and I couldn't keep my eyes open anymore.

# 63

"MORNING," I GROANED, PLODDING INTO THE OFFICE WITH Cinderella underfoot. It was quiet. Oddly quiet. My monitors were dark. My chair unoccupied. My desk looked like a scene straight out of *The Wizard of Oz*, as if it had been swept up by a tornado with papers and manuals thrown all over the place; and beneath it lay Max's legs, sticking out like the Wicked Witch of the East.

"What's happening down there?"

Max peered up over the computer, his hair disheveled, with bloodshot eyes. "I started loading the dailies last night around nine, loaded one drive, and then everything went black. I've been on the phone with techs in Hong Kong and in chat rooms all night trying to fix this."

"Well, this wasn't scheduled."

"I think we are going to need another motherboard," he said as he pulled out a second green board and inspected it.

"A motherboard? How long will that take?" I panicked.

"Let me finish running this last test and I'll know more."

He picked up his flashlight and shined it into the guts of the computer.

The front door opened, blowing in the cool morning air. In piled the camera crew, dragging themselves in from another sixteen-hour night shoot, shuffling across the wooden floor, up the staircase, to sleep the day away only to wake up this afternoon and do it all over again tonight.

*Time for breakfast.*

The sun was up and our street was packed with crew, all scurrying home from the long night of work. Only a handful of us were left in the production department to work the day shift. Cinderella scampered across the floor and leaped into Sunny's lap while I began to grab us some grub.

"Tomorrow is our weekly run to Dali. You sure your visa's good?" Eva asked, while she checked her long list.

"As long as I'm outta China by June 1, I'm good."

I poured another ladle of congee into a bowl.

"According to my schedule, you are leaving the twenty-seventh of April, and that's with a couple of pickup days added at the end, so I guess you're fine."

"We've got problems, I'm afraid." I helped myself to a couple of hard-boiled eggs for Max and the pup and dropped them in my coat pocket. "Our computer is down. Max has been up all night troubleshooting. I think we are going to need to have parts flown in." I stuffed two sticky buns in my other pocket. "Vin may need to go to the airport in Dali tomorrow. I'll let you know when we know more." I picked up the bowls of porridge that I'd filled to the brim and walked back to our office, trying not to spill our breakfast along the way.

Max was talking on the phone while typing in a chat room. I placed his food on the desk. With all that Max had going on, I took my breakfast back to my room. I crawled under the covers and ate the cold boiled rice. Cinderella gobbled up her hard-boiled egg and then joined me on her pillow for a nap.

While I waited for Max to report back on our status, I called Ron. He always knew what to do while we waited. Sometimes we would go for a walk, or play ball, and sometimes we just snuggled. I wished he were here right now. Skype rang and rang and rang and rang.

I finally hung up and looked over at Cinderella.

Asleep on the pillow beside me.

Oblivious to what was happening around her.

Unaware of how to help in an emergency.

*A cappuccino would be really good right now* . . . but Joe's place wasn't open yet. I'd have to wait for him, too.

I looked at the TV I hadn't turned on since I'd been there. Needing a new motherboard triggered old memories.

*On Saturday mornings after Mommy left, Daddy would cook a big breakfast at the crack of dawn. I would roll out my sleeping bag on the green shag carpet in front of the television. With a few of my stuffed animals, I would have my very own Saturday morning slumber party. We'd get into all kinds of trouble with Bugs Bunny, Porky Pig, and Daffy Duck. When Scooby Doo came on and I got scared, I crawled into my sleeping bag, where all my plush pals would protect me until Shaggy and Scooby solved the mystery and all would be safe in the world again, allowing me to jump out of the sleeping bag, which was very important for the next shows because they were the happy family singing shows. The Jacksons, Josie and the Pussycats, and The Monkees. These shows required me to dance and sing along until I needed to lie down from exhaustion.*

*Daddy spent his Saturday mornings at the local Kmart waiting for the next "Blue Light Special." The promotion, held only on Saturday mornings, consisted of a blue flashing police light attached to a metal stick, high enough to be seen above each aisle, on a robot that roamed the store until it landed on merchandise that was "on sale." Then its blue light flashed and spun just like a police car pulling someone over, attracting hordes of people. All bets were off once Daddy heard "Attention Kmart shoppers!" over the PA system. He'd run like a savage, stepping on small children, pushing old ladies over as he raced to the publicized aisle, only to pillage it like a pirate raiding a village, taking what he deemed precious and retreating back to an aisle he'd previously scouted to calculate where the next blue light would twirl.*

*By noon, Daddy arrived home exhausted, looking like Santa Claus with bags full of stuff. He'd take a seat in the living room, pull out each acquired must-have, and share how every "bargain" had been obtained, holding it with such pride, as if he had placed first in every Olympic event he'd entered.*

I stared into the dark TV that hung on the wall, reached for the remote in the drawer of the bedside table, and turned it on.

Chinese opera on one.

Chinese drama on two.

I pressed the channel-down button and it went back to one.

Chinese opera.

Chinese drama on two.

I turned it off.

I couldn't sit still any longer.

I walked back into the office.

The front door had been left open.

I stood inside watching the outside.

An old Chinese man with a basket on his back and three small goats on a rope strolled by.

"I ordered a new motherboard. It should be here tomorrow night."

"There is nothing we can do with my machine down?" I asked.

"I'm afraid not. I'm backing up drives right now from last night's shoot, but they don't need supervision," Max offered up as encouragement that something was getting done.

Just then a six-hundred-pound pig waddled by the front door. She was covered in long black hair and looked as if she had been nursing. Two small baby pigs walked beside her.

"Look, Max." I pointed to the mama pig being led by a petite man.

"It's Friday. That means it's market day," Max said, smiling through his sleepy eyes as he ran his fingers through his hair.

"Market day?" My heart raced. My brain felt giddy. "Fuck it! I wanna shop!"

# 64

BY THE TIME WE GOT TO THE MAIN ROAD, THE STREET HAD TAKEN on a life of its own. Our sleepy village had become quite the hot spot—"market." A group of Naxi women, an ethnic Chinese faction of Tibetan lineage, in their traditional dresses had descended from the surrounding hills for the big day. I felt as if they were going to the ball in Shaxi. They looked so festive in their long black pleated maxi skirts with wide, horizontal stripes of hot pink, fire-engine red, or mint green that skimmed the ground as they walked. Black vests with sequin appliqués of butterflies and flowers topped them off. Every woman wore a hat—not for shade—for decoration. Tiny bowler or mini top hats pinned to their heads with long trailing ribbons in various colors of yarn and beads of beauty.

The street was lined with vendors. The first man we saw wore a headset with a tiny amp the size of a cell phone beside his feet. In the center of his forehead, a Band-Aid. He testified with so much passion and exuded so much faith, one might have mistaken him for an evangelical. He dangled a long strand of Band-Aids while yelling in Mandarin.

"He's selling Band-Aids?" I asked Max, needing confirmation on my deduction skills.

Max listened to the crackling, tinny amp while he shot a few photographs.

"He's selling ten for a yuan."

Next to Band-Aid man stood a display of dentures, a few bottles of salves, and a tray of single teeth, mostly incisors, but I spotted a few random molars in there, too. Both full and partial bridges spread out among the exhibit in all shapes and sizes. *Do they have the tooth fairy there and what was the going rate for a tooth these days?*

A small man in a white coat sat behind the pop-up shop. His large, crooked nose held a pair of much-worn, round wireless glasses. There was a chip in his lower left-hand lens. He smiled at me with a grin that didn't look like any I'd seen since I'd been on the mainland. Then it occurred to me—he had all his teeth. And they were straight, and yet they were all a bit too big for his mouth.

I stared, perhaps a little too long.

Max and I picked up a display item and studied it. I asked him to find out just exactly what went on at this table. Max made his inquiries while I inspected what looked like a lower denture. They went to great lengths here to both tea and tobacco stain fake teeth—a far cry from the Hollywood-perfect pearly whites I had been accustomed to seeing back home.

"He's the village dentist. He comes once a week on Fridays to take care of anyone who needs new teeth." Max flashed his perfect grin at me. "He can have you with a new set in a few weeks."

By now the crowd had become so thick I didn't like having Cinderella on a leash, fearing she might bite someone, so I reached down to pick her up, and Max placed her in the basket on my back.

Eggplant, bok choy, cabbage, and corn had all been laid out on the ground for shoppers to pick and choose. Large baskets of garlic and red peppers lined our path. An old lady displayed knives, arranging them from smallest to largest on a bright red cloth, while she sat on a wooden box, eating her breakfast from a bowl with chopsticks. I wondered how she transported such sharp objects back and forth to the market every week without cutting herself.

Another old lady stopped to study the knives while she gabbed away, holding her cell phone in one hand with a live rooster tucked under her other arm. I asked Max to take her photo—this was not something I was used to seeing every day.

I caught her catching a glimpse of me with Cinderella in my basket on my back. Obviously, something she was not used to seeing every day either.

The market became packed.

Bodies everywhere.

Shoving and pushing.

I was getting knocked around. It became harder and harder to move, like being on the subway at rush hour. *Where are all these people coming from?* I'd never seen them before and they certainly didn't live in this tiny village.

I stumbled over a large bag of tea.

So much loose tea.

Jasmine tea.

Green tea.

White tea.

Tea and more tea.

Next to those stood smaller sacks of spices.

Oranges, reds, and greens.

Leaves, seeds, and flowers.

Mesmerizing.

A kaleidoscope so stimulating, yet disorienting.

I looked around for Max but couldn't find him in the crowd. I knew he was close by, so I kept moving in the flow of people, passing baskets of Asian pears, clementines, melons, and green bananas. People with baskets on their back, like bumper cars bouncing into each other.

Eventually the crowd began to funnel out as it opened into a large, gated area where steel vats held live fish.

Shoppers filled plastic bags with the catch of their choice and then they were weighed. I watched as a man negotiated a lower price.

The seller shook his head.

Then the buyer shook his head.

Back and forth.

Back and forth.

It made me think of my daddy and how he loved a bargain.

*Daddy's bargaining began before he arrived at the market. His began before sunup, after the morning paper arrived. He'd peruse the supermarket section, taking notes in his small flip notebook, the kind detectives on cop shows often carried and which held important details that needed to be referred back to at a later date.*

*Wednesdays, Saturdays, and Sundays were the papers my father lived for. They held what Charlie from Charlie and the Chocolate Factory called "The Golden Tickets"—coupons.*

*My father loved coupons.*

*He loved the hunt for coupons, clipping coupons, and sorting coupons. Then hunting through his sorted coupons, finding the ones he needed, scouting out the items. The Grand Finale: presenting the coupons to the cashier where he received his white ribbon—the receipt that two trees had given their lives for. He'd scroll down his award to read the deductions like a CPA, pleased with all he'd saved.*

*Now, most of what he had purchased was not what a kid of nine deemed edible, but Daddy didn't care. He'd saved money and happily ate whatever corn chip and dip he purchased as long as it had come with a coupon.*

When I found Max again, he was at the weigh station, photographing the transactions. He looked wired yet exhausted. His bloodshot eyes needed some shut-eye.

Just outside the fish area, I spotted a van with a canvas—double doors in the back that were wide open. One very long-necked goose stood next to a much shorter-necked goose. Both peered out as customers walked by. They looked like they could have been right out of a Beatrix Potter storybook, going out for a ride in the country to visit Peter Rabbit and Mrs. Tiggy-Winkle. And then I remembered where I was. I tried not to think of their fate—someone's dinner table.

"Come on, Max. You need to get some sleep," I said, rescuing myself from my dark thoughts.

# 65

IT WAS STILL DARK OUTSIDE—THAT EARLY-MORNING, INKY-BLUE sky just before dawn breaks.

I peered through the glass door into our office.

The light was on—the parts had arrived—the machine was up and running.

Max sat hunched over at my desk, neck craned up to the monitor while he double-checked the scene number against the script notes. His furrowed brow and the slowness of his manner told me he had not been to bed yet, and I wondered when he'd last had any sleep.

"You are a genius, Max."

"We're all caught up from the last two days. But they just sent three more drives." He took a breath, letting out a long yawn without one hint of complaint. I'd never worked with anyone like him—an Energizer Bunny who had just taken a licking but kept on ticking.

Cinderella bounced over to Max, bringing him a moment of joy as he smiled while he patted her head.

"Breakfast is served in a few minutes. Want anything?"

"No. I need a break. I'll get this next drive set up and run over myself."

My mind wandered to all the things we needed to do to catch up. Truth was, we were at least four days behind. Being down two days had put us further behind. Things moved so much slower in Yunnan. Definitely slower than in Hollywood. And there wasn't much I could do about that. We were already working around the clock.

The cold air hit my neck as I opened the door, making me pull my scarf farther up around my neck with one hand, and with Cinderella's leash in my other hand, I closed the door behind us. As I pulled the scarf tighter around my neck, I snagged my foot on the edge of a box that had been left in the middle of the stoop, falling to the ground—catching myself with my hands before I fell face-first onto the cement.

I rolled over.

Cinderella looked at me—cocked her head to one side and then the other.

I looked at my hands and sat up, making a quick assessment. No broken bones or skinned knees. I heaved a heavy sigh of relief and then looked over in the box. It was a fruit box, like the one you would find in the market without a lid. As I peered over the edge, I saw a tiny white puppy, asleep.

Cinderella gazed over the top, her nose working double time as she took short sniffs around the furry baby's body. I looked both ways down the street to see if I could spot who had left her, but the street was empty. Down by the square, I could hear they had begun wrapping last night's shoot.

I scooted closer so I could pick her up. A girl—so small she fit in the palm of my hand. I moved her up to my chest for warmth and she started to stir. She started stretching her front paws, then her back ones—her little legs the size of my thumbs.

Cinderella danced in place, adjusting herself to the new smell while I watched the puppy's little rib cage move up and down with each breath she took. She had no business being away from her mother yet. My nose started to tingle, and not the good kind of tingle. The kind that is followed by raining eyes. There was no way this little one could make it on her own. Dumped and left in the cold. To me, this little creature was a precious newborn, to be loved and placed in my baby carriage with the rest of my special babies.

A downpour of tears drenched my face. I cried so loud the puppy opened her eyes, so I hugged her closer. Cinderella did her best to snuggle with us while I bathed the little one in tears and snot.

# 66

ACTORS DRESSED IN COSTUMES FOR THE BALL FROM THE NIGHT shoot, the entire crew passing me; Mandarin everywhere, Cinderella's lead on my wrist as I held the puppy close.

The crowd grew thicker leaving the set, hungry and tired from a sixteen-hour night shoot.

I walked against the pack. Bumped up against their shoulders, like a passenger at the back of the plane trying to get to the front when it's boarding. Hordes of people kept coming. Cinderella's lead got tangled around legs. I reached down to pick her up.

Heads and feet.

More Mandarin.

By the time we rounded the corner, the crowd had thinned out. A few people still lingered, most of them around the camera, talking to Robert. I waited, watching Wang Lee and Robert discuss the night shoot through Robert's translator. Robert's hair had grown grayer since the last time I saw him. His jeans hung loosely from his skinny frame. He looked over in my direction.

"Lisa?"

"I didn't know where to go or what to do." My voice cracked.

Robert looked at the helpless puppy in my hand.

"Someone left this little one in a box on my front stoop this morning. Who could have abandoned such a sweet little being?"

"Somebody who knew you'd look after it, that's who."

*I haven't even found a home for Cinderella yet. And we're leaving in a couple weeks.*

Robert mustered a smile and turned back to his translator. His eyelids kept closing while he listened as they walked toward another part of the set.

I looked down at the baby, so small and helpless, trying to digest what Robert had just said.

"You didn't hear anything outside the window last night when you were working?"

Max lifted his head out of his bowl of porridge. "No, why?"

"Because I found this." I lowered the puppy so Max could see her sweet face.

"Another dog!" Sunny shrilled, jumping up from the table as she clapped her hands together.

"Wait, what?" Max asked, shaking his head.

"There was a box on the stoop this morning and she was in it."

Her big brown eyes stared up at him as he reached over to hold our latest crew member. He had been hesitant when I brought Cinderella in the van that day, especially after she threw up, but this one was so little, his natural instincts took over.

"She's so tiny," he said as he gently inspected her.

"I want to hold her! I want to hold her!" Sunny demanded as she jumped up and down.

Max carefully handed her to Sunny while I studied her

miniature white body. Despite its size, it was stout and sturdy. Legs close to the ground. Wide and stump-like. Her transparent nails were visible and long. On her lower back, just above her rump, was a light brown spot in the shape of a heart with the pointy side of the heart facing her tail. She had a square face and two triangle ears, which folded over like a pita bread sandwich that matched the color of her heart marking. She couldn't have weighed more than four pounds.

*Sweet. So, so sweet.*

"I think we should name her Mei Mei after our hero in the movie so she gets a happily ever after," I suggested.

"Mei Mei!" Sunny emoted. "Yes, Mei Mei!"

Eva looked up from petting Mei Mei and nodded. "Great name, but what are we going to do with her?"

"First we need to feed her, but I'm not sure what." I looked over at the breakfast table and inspected the half-eaten food. "Let's start with some congee."

"I gotta check on the dailies." Max jumped up out of his seat. "I'll bring Cinderella's bowls over."

I'd learned the day I rescued Cinderella that none of the crew had ever had a dog, which meant no one knew how to care for one—much less a puppy. "I think we should give Mei Mei some milk."

"I'll ask Joe," Max said as he walked in with Cinderella's dishes.

"Of course, my dealer, Coffee Joe. He takes care of my coffee latte fix—he'll know where to score milk."

*Max—always the problem solver.*

# 67

NOW THERE WERE THREE OF US AT MY DESK EACH DAY—ME
and "my girls."

Cinderella sat on top of her basket, giving her the best view
of the room. Mei Mei slept in my lap while I screened the dailies.
It was lonely with the entire crew sleeping all day and working
all night, but I had the girls to keep me company. Max worked
the night shift, backing up drives and loading dailies while I
worked from early morning until after dinner assembling new
scenes. Each day felt like Groundhog Day. The only thing that
changed was the scene I was cutting.

Every night the three of us would fall into bed. Cinderella
shared her pillow with Mei Mei now. I always thought about
Ron before I turned out the light—hoping he knew it wouldn't
be long before I was home.

# 68

WHILE MAX WAS TELLING ME WE HAD A "DRIVE PROBLEM," I started to feel lightheaded. A sharp pain shot up the back of my neck and began wrapping itself around my forehead like a boa constrictor devouring its prey. Rubbing my neck didn't seem to help. I studied the shooting schedule. It had been a grueling one even if everything had gone without a hitch.

*We're already a week behind and now we've got more tech problems?*

"Now what?" I asked while everything was becoming more and more blurry.

"I'm having to transfer footage to an additional drive, so it's taking twice as long."

"Robert wanted to see another scene today. Am I going to be able to show him something? Anything?" I begged.

I opened the garden door. Cinderella and Mei Mei ran in. I reached for the doorjamb, trying to steady myself. The front door blew open. In dragged the guys from another sixteen-hour day.

*More footage arriving.*

*We'll never catch up.*

I opened my eyes and saw Wang Lee.

"Nǐ . . . Nǐ hǎoooo."

He and the room went out of focus. My body teetered back and forth before my knees gave way and I collapsed onto the cold, hard stone floor.

"Liiiiiiiisaaaaaaa!!!" Max shouted.

Frantic footsteps.

Mandarin.

Rustling.

Hands.

Arms.

*I'm okay. I'm okay. I just need a hand up.*

My mouth never opened.

Not a word came out.

Gardenias. I could smell gardenias.

I opened my eyes.

Blurry.

I blinked.

I blinked again.

Wang Lee, his fingers on my wrist.

I took a deep breath in, exhaled, and nodded.

"Can you hear me? Lisa?" Max looked down at me with a furrowed brow. "You fainted. We carried you to your room." He hadn't looked this worried since we'd met. Even when the motherboard died.

Wang Lee spoke.

Max interpreted. "You have a very low pulse."

Wang Lee nodded.

Max looked at me with laser-focused eyes. He shook his head as if to scold me. "Wang Lee has Chinese herbs, or . . . you can go to the hospital."

I shook my head. "No! No hospital!"

Max knew what I meant. Everyone at the hospital here received the same exact treatment no matter what was wrong with them—a saline drip.

Max translated for Wang Lee.

*I got sick.*

*Really sick.*

*The summer after my sister was born, Daddy was transferred back to the States. He had planned a big trip for us to see the world on our way back.*

*I was so sick I couldn't walk.*

*We stopped and spent time in Dublin, where I stayed in the hotel room and watched Tarzan movies while Mommy and Daddy explored Ireland.*

*We had to cut our trip short.*

*We flew back to the States to stay with my grandparents in Chapel Hill, where I went to Duke for all kinds of tests. They even did a spinal tap. They said I had pneumonia of the kidneys, whatever that means.*

*In Chinese medicine, the kidneys are related to fear and anxiety.*

"I will make you a cup of hot tea with Wang Lee's Chinese herbs." Max picked up my kettle and filled it. "You must rest, Lisa."

"Max, *you* must rest."

"I will. Soon."

"Where are Cinderella and Mei Mei?"

"Look."

There they were, right beside me on their pillow—my girls.

"I will feed them once I take care of you."

"*Shay shay*, Max," I whispered, feeling nurtured and cared for by these men, who were more exhausted than I was. I felt special, even princess-like, being made a magic potion and letting them take care of me—and my baby girls.

# 69

MUCH TO MY RELIEF, AFTER DRINKING WANG LEE'S OTHERWORLDLY herbs and a much-needed nap, I returned to my desk.

Today's scene: Mei Mei is held captive by the king's men.

I worked slow and steady while the camera crew slept until almost dark.

Wang Lee checked on me as promised, taking my pulse. Again, he diagnosed it too low. More magical potion.

Max relieved me earlier than usual. We were still behind schedule, but being taken care of in a way I had never been before made me feel better.

*I had to be sick, like fever sick or throw-up sick, in order to stay home from school. When we moved to Newton, North Carolina, Daddy dropped my sister off at day care before work. I walked a block to school myself, so if I got sick and had to stay home, there was no one to take care of me. And if I did, I had to stay in bed. I wasn't allowed to watch TV—not that there was anything good to watch during the day back then with only three TV channels.*

Daddy would come home for lunch and cook Campbell's tomato soup and a grilled cheese sandwich made from Wonder Bread and Velveeta cheese. He'd play card games with me—War or Spit. And board games—Checkers or Mancala. Even when I was younger, he beat me at Chutes and Ladders and Candy Land. He got great satisfaction beating a child at a game. He could care less his kid was a loser—he just cared that he emerged victorious.

He loved winning.

It made me competitive, very competitive.

# 70

"BYE-BYE," I SAID TO SHOE LADY AS SHE OPENED HER SHOP, revealing all the beautiful slippers that would one day find their perfect feet. With Cinderella on my back, and my arms wrapped around Mei Mei's very own basket, I was leaving Shaxi with my two best friends still in need of finding their forever homes.

One last location. A day's drive away.

Bright yellow flowers blanketing both sides of the road.

We sped through the countryside—the hypnotic rhythm of the tires reminded me of the farmland and cow pastures I passed as a kid on trips with my father.

*Daddy loved the adventure of a road trip and took me to see my grandparents whenever possible. This meant a twelve-hour nonstop drive in our olive-green wood-paneled Plymouth station wagon. Daddy liked to get up at three thirty to be on the road by four. All our packing had to be done the night before, including meals. Sandwiches were Daddy's food of choice—allowing him to eat with one hand and drive with the other. His sandwich: peanut butter, banana, and mayo.*

*Mine: peanut butter and Marshmallow Fluff. Both on Wonder Bread.*

*Daddy made us eat a bowl of cereal before we hit the road. We weren't allowed to leave the house on an empty stomach. I was in charge of the grocery bag filled with all kinds of snacks that I passed out upon demand.*

*I copiloted from the back of the wagon, inside my sleeping bag with a cooler the size of our refrigerator filled to the brim with ice, discounted sodas, and beer. Daddy loved Faygo Red Pop and whatever beer that had been on sale. Me, I liked Dr Pepper and tried not to drink too much because Daddy had a thing about stopping. He was on a mission and it didn't include bathroom breaks.*

When I opened my eyes, we were now hanging over the edge of a cliff that dropped off miles above the Yangtze River.

It was so steep I could only see the drop-off below.

There were no guard railings.

No barriers to prevent us from falling.

The switchbacks were tighter than a paper clip.

I grabbed the handle above the passenger window as we skimmed the rim, scaling the mountain, back and forth, hanging like trapeze artists.

With the calmness of a bomb expert and the focus of a tightrope walker, Vin rode the edge of that cliff with the speed of a race car driver. On occasion, a vehicle approached us head-on. I'm still not exactly sure how Vin maneuvered the passing of another car.

We eventually made it to the bottom of the mountain—Cinderella predictably threw up on an old newspaper I had packed for her—before we pulled up in front of a red and black building with a big picture window. The crew was already seated at two large family-style tables—Wang Lee in his flat cap, sipping a beer.

In front of the restaurant an old woman squatted, washing dishes in a pan of water, dipping a tiny teacup and splashing it around. She didn't use any soap. Just water. While I contemplated the sanitation of this joint, it occurred to me: I'd just made it down the side of a mountain in a van on a road the width of a bicycle lane.

*I'm going to be fine—just fine—dining here.*

A little girl with pigtails in pink ribbons sat at an empty table, shucking peas.

"You don't look so good," Eva said as she handed me a cup of ginger tea. "This should make you feel better."

Camaraderie filled the room.

So much joy and laughter.

My heart was full and so was my bladder. I finished the entire pot of ginger tea knowing I would be asking Vin to make a few more stops along the way.

# 71

clouds moved through the Tiffany-blue sky above, creating in-the-moment masterpieces. A cloud in the shape of a heart morphed into a teddy bear, then transformed into a dog scampering across the sky.

Our one-lane road widened into parked vans and buses. Vin pulled alongside them.

"Stone City has furniture like beds and desks and even pillows built out of stone."

"Stone? Pillows?"

Max leaned in between the bucket seats, nodding. "At least that's what Vin told me."

"With my back and neck, I was hoping the beds were going to be a little more comfortable?"

Not only were there a few bruises left from my fainting spell, it was even harder to move my neck since then. I was so exhausted. I'd never worked this hard for this long—my body just gave out.

We each brought just the necessities at this location; everything needed to be carried down the side of the mountain. My two big suitcases would stay in the van, waiting until my plane trip home. Two dozen local women, who had been hired by the film, milled about until they found "the item" they would carry, then strapped it to their backs for the hike down to Stone City.

A woman my age in a thick pullover sweater padded the large anvil case on her back. The case weighed as much as she did.

Watching these women filled me with awe . . . and pain.

"Well done!" Robert greeted me. "You made it to the last location! And I see you brought your new friends." He petted Cinderella and Mei Mei and pointed to the two donkeys at the beginning of the trail. "I reserved one for you."

"Need a hand up?" Max asked.

*So this is happening.*

I was taken aback but didn't dare complain. I was one of two lucky enough to hitch a ride while the rest of the crew had to traverse the mountain on foot.

"No, thank you. I can do this." I hoisted myself up, swinging one leg over, and grabbed the donkey's neck before sliding off the other side. There were no stirrups. No saddle. No reins. Just a blanket between me and the sweet beast who would carry us. Cinderella lay across the donkey's neck and Mei Mei sat in the crux of my arm.

Stone City was built on a rock that looked like a mushroom. We tacked back and forth on a long dirt path against the mountain, slow and steady, while Robert's donkey led the way. On occasion, when our donkeys were close enough, he'd shout out the history of Stone City to me.

"This is an old Naxi town. Kublai Khan rested here during one of his battles." And then, his voice trailed off as he rode out ahead of us.

This was the land of kingdoms, struggle, and strife.

A train of women, like a centipede, carried everything from props to camera equipment down the side of the massive mountain. I was curious as to why men weren't doing this. Maybe there weren't any in this village. I had heard there were villages without men.

Directly behind us, a woman led a horse loaded with firewood. But not the big, thick wood that needed to be split with an axe. Long, skinny sticks that would be used for cooking in a kitchen. Cinderella slept on the donkey's neck. Motion sickness escaped her on this part of the journey.

# 72

WHEN WE FINALLY REACHED THE ENTRANCE TO STONE CITY, it looked like something out of a fairy tale. The stone pathway changed into a staircase that led to the entrance—a tall gray archway with two turrets, one on each side.

There were only two entrances to Stone City, this being the main one. Warriors dreamed of being protected behind such a fortress.

Max had found the owner of our guesthouse, a petite woman with a pixie haircut and a baby girl in a blanket strapped to her back, who led us through the main gate and up the dirt road. While they chatted, I pondered the name "Stone City."

I thought of New York City.

Kansas City.

Oklahoma City.

*This is the furthest thing from a city I've ever seen.*

The closest car was an hour donkey ride away. I hadn't even passed a shoe or coffee shop. This wasn't even a town or a village.

As we passed through an old wooden gate, Max said, "This is Ping, our hostess. She said one hundred families live here."

Ping opened a door, where we stepped onto a large stone

patio that ran to the edge of the cliff, protected by a waist-high wall. On one side of the patio sat a card table with four men smoking cigarettes, drinking beer, and playing mahjong.

That's where the men were. While women were lugging the baggage, the men were partying. All four of them.

The four heads looked up. One man reached for his beer and took a swig; another took a long, slow drag off his filter-less cigarette, held it in his lungs for what seemed like an eternity, and then disappeared in the cloud of smoke as he exhaled. The third sat like a statue in a blue bucket hat. The last man glared at our hostess.

Just beyond the greeting committee sat a stack of firewood piled high and a large black pot on an open fire. At the far end stood a spacious chicken coop, and past the open-air kitchen was a wooden staircase that led to the second floor.

There was a room with a bath for me. Max would share a room with the soundman. The camera crew would stay in a much larger guesthouse.

We stood on the balcony between our rooms, overlooking the Yangtze River.

"So where is our office this week?" I asked.

Max gazed at the mythic view before us.

"We could set up a table right here."

With the mountains and clouds before me, there was no better view. Besides, I'd never had an outside edit bay.

Max clapped his hands together as if to say, "Good," and was off and running.

Mei Mei wandered onto the balcony. I picked her up and held her close to my chest as I watched the world below.

Ping climbed the stairs with her daughter still strapped to

her back and dropped off a snack for her five-year-old son who was doing his schoolwork before she went back to work in the kitchen, all the while taking care of the mahjong men.

I thought of all the women who had carried our equipment down the mountain and into our guesthouses. The women worked so hard here.

The late afternoon shadows fell over the stoic mountains before me. They were long and moved fast across the giant mountains and through the valley. Dried corn cobs and salted ham in white cloth bags hung above my new edit table. A sight I had never seen before and would never see again.

I took a seat in my chair and began sorting through the day's dailies.

# 73

THE CREW LEFT BEFORE DAYLIGHT AND HIKED DOWN TO THE river, where they would camp in tents for the next three days. I slept until dawn.

Letting the girls out in the morning required a lot more work than in Shaxi. It meant a flight of stairs, going across the large patio, and then outside for a walk—never a person in sight. A black-and-gray-striped cat often passed our path—she'd move quickly, having somewhere to be. Surprisingly, the girls didn't seem bothered by her. Back home, we had a kitten the next block over and Ron played with her. It was the only other animal I ever saw him really play with. We were both selective in who we chose to spend our time with.

Morning walks like this reminded me of him.

I missed him.

Entering the house on the first morning, I saw a whole side of the downstairs I didn't notice because I was so distracted by the mahjong men.

Across from the mahjong table, underneath our bedrooms and balcony, was a store with a pool table. The shelves were messy and unorganized, but there did seem to be some sort of a system.

On the top shelf: one kind of liquor stacked with half a dozen boxes.

Below, sodas in plastic bottles.

On another: lots of tiny boxes and things wrapped in plastic like tissues, dental needs, and other bathroom stuff.

In front stood a freezer. It opened from the top and you had to lean in to get what was kept inside—like the kind that held ice cream I remembered from being a kid. This looked like Stone City's 7-Eleven.

I inspected the pool table. It looked like every pool table I'd ever seen in any bar I'd ever been into. The balls were racked and ready for a game.

I thought about the poor donkey who carried it down the mountain.

# 74

The dampness in the air made it feel colder as I sat on the balcony in my outside office. With my hands donning Mavis's gloves and my scarf wrapped tight, I took in the lush colors— a masterpiece in nature. Saturated in mist, the mountains became a deep velvety brown, less jagged and harsh, soft like a watercolor. Terraced lime-green rice fields bathed in drizzle with golden yellow flowers sprinkled throughout. Far below, the swirling blueish-green Yangtze rushed along the banks, forceful and impatient, on its way to its next destination.

Ping, her daughter strapped on her back, busied herself downstairs. The black cauldron cooked while she swept and gathered eggs from the chicken coop. Whenever I was working above, Ping was working below.

Today's scene: Mei Mei's arrival to the ball.

Mei Mei stands under the archway entrance of the square.

The gown: navy, with short cap sleeves.

The bodice: fitted, sewn with pieces of silver that flared into a mini bubble skirt.

A lavender collar topped it off, edged in silver coins.

Her headpiece: a navy bucket hat. Strands of silver beads hung like a veil in front of her face.

On her feet, the heirloom goldfish slippers. Ribbons wrapped her legs from her ankles to her knees.

I sorted all the footage, selected my favorite takes, and began to work the scene, cutting it in all the ways I could imagine.

When I looked up to give my eyes a break, I saw Max with the man who had hiked up from the river carrying the latest footage. Every day, rain or shine, the film arrived. In his khaki hat, he would hike back down the mountain, wait until the last shot of the day, and then hike back up at night with more footage, only to do the same thing all over again tomorrow.

I wondered about the crew and how they were surviving this cold, wet weather, sleeping in tents along the river, cooking on a campfire with only the food they were able to carry down.

*I* had a warm room with a bed where Ping cooked three meals a day for me plus an office with a view.

Life was good where I was.

# 75

WHEN THE HAZE AND DRIZZLE VANISHED, THE MAHJONG game resumed in full swing below with another table next it. Four additional men playing cards.

Ping pinned wet clothes to a clothesline. She looked up at me and smiled.

I began cutting the beginning of the dance. Starting with a wide shot of the square in Shaxi, panning to the ball attendees, to close-ups of the girls in their fancy dresses. Each girl's dress was sewn in tiny pieces of silver—all to display her wealth. Their families stood on the sidelines with dowries, ready to marry them off. The band played from the opera house above as the girls begin to dance in a circle around a huge bonfire. A dance they had all practiced—one they had waited their whole lives to dance.

Ping escorted two women down the balcony, each lugging her own backpack. They stood in silence behind me and watched while I worked on my laptop.

I played a roughed-out scene of Mei Mei joining the circle dance while the prince, hiding behind a big wooden door, watches. No one knows the prince is at the dance. As I watched the playback, I heard one of the women whisper in Mandarin.

*Does she like the cut from the wide shot to the close-up?*
*Does she prefer lingering on the wide?*
*Did she go to a dance to find her husband?*
*Did she have to show all her assets in order to get a spouse?*

Before I had time to ask, they were gone. I peered over the balcony, hoping to catch them, but they'd vanished.

I watched Ping. Her daughter now walked behind her, stumbling as she tried to keep up. She couldn't have been more than two, wanting to help her mother in the kitchen. Ping placed a pot in front of her and handed her a wooden spoon. The baby mimicked her mother by putting her spoon in the pot and stirring.

I watched this sweet woman doing what I could not begin to do.

Clean out the chicken coop.

School her children.

Tend to her husband.

Day in and day out.

I wondered what my life would have been like had I married my high school boyfriend, Harry, who proposed to me in the back seat of his '77 Trans Am.

I thought of my college boyfriend, Spencer, whom I dated for seven years. Spencer proposed with an amethyst ring in a box of Valentine's chocolates.

There would be three more proposals after that.

All I would not accept.

None of them could I see raising a child with, much less spending the rest of my life with.

# 76

"WE ELOPED!" MAVIS GIGGLED AS SHE HELD UP HER WEDDING band to the camera.

"Wow! Congratulations!"

"Yep," she said as she exhaled into a cloud of smoke. "We put Sugar Ray and Ron Howard in the back seat, drove to Vegas, went through the drive-thru with the Elvis impersonator . . . And just like that . . . we're married. There are four of us in the bed now."

"I'm so happy for you."

"Me, too. It's all about timing. We met thirty years ago and we just weren't ready then—but we are now. You ready to come home in a few days?"

"Am I ever."

# 77

This meant packing up Cinderella's basket to help her adjust to her new home. I put one hundred yen aside as a dowry for each of the girls. After Cinderella was all packed up, I sat on the floor and held them both in my lap one last time while they drifted off to sleep.

I watched their little bodies move up and down as they took in each breath until their bodies synced and moved as one.

I wanted to photograph that moment, but I would have to remember it.

*I hope Cinderella remembers me.*

Mei Mei's tiny white body with tan markings had grown thanks to a steady diet of nutrition and affection, now a sweet sight spooned against Cinderella's black fur. She was going to miss Cinderella the most, I feared. Cinderella had been her mommy and now I was separating them. I felt happiness and sadness. Sunny bounded down the balcony with the luminance of her name that radiated from her being.

"Cinderella!" Sunny gasped. The excitement of getting her very own dog was palpable. I'd bottle it if I could.

We hugged.

"I miss her already, but I know you two will have a happily ever after and that makes me *wǒ gǎndào hěn kāixīn*."

"I promise to take good care of her. I will walk her and feed her and play with her every day. You don't need to worry about her."

*I'm more worried about me without her.*

Cinderella jumped up into Sunny's arms. It was indeed a match made in fairy-tale land.

I handed Sunny Cinderella's leash.

"*Wǒ gǎndào hěn kāixīn. Wǒ gǎndào hěn kāixīn.*"

# 78

I ZIPPED UP MY CARRY-ON, LIFTED IT OFF THE TABLE, AND looked around the room one last time. It looked like it did when I arrived. Double bed, nightstand, and a small table that looked out a picture window. So simple, but the view: spectacular!

Tomorrow I would spend the day in Lijiang getting massages.

Vin collected my carry-on and joined Max, who was already at the main gate, leaving just the two of us. I carried Mei Mei down the wooden staircase past the chicken coop, through the open-air kitchen to the gambling area.

"*Shay shay.*" I nodded as I passed by the mahjong men for the last time. Husband, never looking up, placed a tile on the board with one hand while he waved with his other, uttering, "Bye-bye."

Ping and her children lined up next to the front door.

"*Shay shay,*" I said while I made eye contact with Ping. I put my hand on my heart muttering "*Shay shay*" again. It brought tears to my eyes how hard she worked, and I wondered, did anyone else even notice how she spent her day? What she did to make their day better? I wanted her to know that what she did every day made her Superwoman.

I placed Mei Mei on the ground and smiled at the children. The two tiny tots reached down to pet her with a giggle and then they turned to look back up at me.

"Bye-bye," they said in unison as they waved their small hands.

I took one good look into those sweet faces and wondered: Would they leave Stone City or would they stay and raise their children like their parents had? Would the little boy run the mahjong table with the view? Would the little girl marry a boy from Stone City?

Before I began my walk to the main gate, I stopped to take a look at the last guesthouse I would visit in Yunnan. From this side of the house, you'd never know the breathtaking view on the other side.

I thought about the stories Robert told as we traveled down the mountain. How Stone City was the only village along the Yangtze that Kublai Khan had not destroyed on his vast rampage.

I peered down a tiny alleyway, where a small brown dog lay sleeping, soaking up the morning sunshine.

Max greeted us at the main gate.

"I'm going to miss you terribly, Max. Two days on my own. Who will translate for me?"

"You'll be fine in Lijiang without me. You need to rest."

"'Thank you' doesn't begin to cover all you have done for me." I hugged Max, not wanting to let him go as my eyes began to water up. "*Shay shay*, Max."

"I will see you in Los Angeles in a week and you will show me all of Hollywood. I can't wait! I've never been to America before!"

Wang Lee arrived at the gate with his bags. He stacked them on top of the other luggage waiting to be transported up the mountain.

"Wang Lee!"

As he approached me, I smiled and stared into his twinkling eyes. "*Shay shay*, Wang Lee. *Shay shay*."

He nodded and then flashed me his signature grin.

I studied his charming smile, his closely trimmed hair, topped with his trademark flat cap, as I thought back to Shaxi, where we'd shared a house together, danced together, thrown cake, and dined together. Wang Lee had nursed me back to health that fateful day.

Not a word was spoken.

We stood still.

Just one more moment.

Allowing the connection of one human to honor the presence of another.

Honored to have met him, if only for the briefest of time.

Knowing I would never see him again and that my life would be forever changed having lived with Wang Lee, and his crew of twelve men, in a guesthouse in Shaxi.

# 79

Mei Mei and I stayed in the van while Vin checked me in. I studied every inch of her one last time. *My baby*: searing every detail into memory—from her broad pink nose with its tiny black mustache-like marking to the two caramel-colored, wide paintbrush strokes on top of her head, topped off with the café au lait–colored heart on her rear.

Vin handed me the room key, followed close behind with one suitcase, and went back for the other.

"*Shay shay*," I said to him as he put down the second suitcase. I hugged Mei Mei tight. "You are about to start the biggest adventure with the most wonderful little boy."

Vin looked at me. I looked at him and then back to Mei Mei, telling her, "Vin's boy is seven, almost my age when I got my first puppy."

Mei Mei had been a gift from someone who knew I would love her and care for her the way she deserved . . . who knew I would find the perfect home for her.

I walked over and handed her to Vin.

"*Shay shay*, Vin. *Shay shay*." I stepped forward to hug them both.

Vin didn't hug back.

I didn't want to let go.

"Bye-bye, my friends." I began to weep.

"Bye-bye," Vin said, and then he and Mei Mei vanished down the stairway and into the crowd below.

I sobbed for Mei Mei.

I sobbed for Cinderella.

I sobbed . . . and sobbed . . . for having the opportunity to love and care for them.

For the joy they brought me and the joy they would bring their new families.

For the crew I spent so much time with, who never spoke to me but who taught me to keep being me no matter how old I was and that I would find my tribe no matter where I went.

But most of all, I sobbed knowing that I'd never see any of them ever again.

# 80

IT FELT GOOD TO SLEEP THROUGH THE NIGHT AND NOT WAKE UP until the sun came up, to have nowhere to be and nothing to do. I'd fantasized about this moment for three months and fourteen days—and it was finally here. I was still in yesterday's clothes, and hungry. After a shower, I was ready to start my first day without having to cut to scene. Without having to work 'til I dropped. My time was my own.

Lijiang was a night town, so most of the shops and restaurants were closed. I popped into the first and only stall I found open. An old man mopped the floor. He wiped his hands on his black Chinese jacket and spoke to me in Mandarin. I pantomimed eating. He returned five minutes later, serving me a bowl of congee with a fried egg on top. While I dined, I watched Lijiang wake up—merchants scurried past, carrying bags and moving carts as they began their day. Across the way, a large wooden door opened. The vendor, a young girl dressed in a red fake-fur coat, set up her display tables outside.

After breakfast, I went to check out the tables. I found a basket of wooden beaded prayer bracelets, each bead etched with a different Chinese character. Several small knots tied to look like a flower held the bracelets together.

The saleswoman brought out more bracelets in baskets—

these were made from colored stones. Mostly green and pink.

"How much?"

"Twenty yuan," she replied. "Prayer beads. Very sacred."

She'd obviously been taught great sales English, so I held up both hands and said, "Ten, please."

"Ten?" she questioned. "Ah . . . you get good deal."

"*Shay shay.*" I smiled.

"One hundred and sixty. I give you good price," she affirmed as she handed me a bag. "I give you better price on these," she said as she held up a gemstone bracelet.

"No, thank you. Just these."

"I give you best price in Lijiang," she said with a smile.

"No. *Shay shay.*"

"Okay. Bye-bye."

Across from the bracelet store, I spotted a massage sign with an arrow pointing up to the second story. At the top of the stairs, I opened a red door. A spry middle-aged woman dressed in a red T-shirt and black knit pants entered from behind a red velvet curtain. She rattled off something in Mandarin.

"*Nǐ hǎo.* Massage for two hours, please," I said while I held up two fingers. She muttered something in Mandarin while mirroring back two fingers.

"Sixty yuan," she said, pointing to the sign in Mandarin behind her. She motioned me to follow her beyond the curtain, which led to a very large room with low cots a foot off the ground. Each cot was separated by a curtain for privacy. No one removed their clothing in China for a massage, unlike in the States. Fully dressed, I lay face down and waited.

Another woman appeared. She muttered a few things in Mandarin.

"*Shay shay*" was all I knew, having no idea what she just conveyed.

She rubbed my neck. It hurt and felt good at the same time. Between sitting and craning while staring at a monitor nonstop for three months, my shoulders felt as if they had become one with my earlobes. Every part of my body needed kneading. She moved down my upper back to my lower back. At one point she chopped with the sides of her hands. Circulation started to flow again. She worked her way down to my feet, working each pressure point until it lulled me to sleep.

She shook one shoulder and said, "Finish," with a big smile.

I opened my eyes and looked at her. She was missing two lower front teeth. I pulled ten yuan out of my pocket for a tip and laid it on the bed.

"*Shay shay*," I said, feeling wobbly from the release of my muscles. "*Wǒ gǎndào hěn kāixīn.*" I heard her giggle at my Mandarin, which, clearly, I'd far from mastered, while I walked down the staircase.

The sun was shining bright, right into my eyes. I reached for my sunglasses and slowly walked down the uneven pathway. By now, people were milling everywhere. I took a seat at a table in a tiny coffee stand.

Hearing the grinding of the beans made me inhale the aroma, like Pavlov's dogs.

I pulled out Ron's tennis ball and gave it a squeeze.

*I wonder what he's doing?*

*Does he know I'm coming home?*

*How's Sunny?*

*Is Cinderella behaving?*

*And sweet Mei Mei. Her round, pudgy baby body. I'll miss*

*watching her walk across the floor and the way she curled up next to Cinderella.*

Coffee and massages—it didn't get more decadent than that. I downed my first cappuccino so could I order another.

After my second cappuccino, it was time for my second massage. I stumbled into the closest one I could find—upstairs, two doors down. The receiving room was small, just a love seat covered in red fabric with black Chinese characters. A small fountain sat on a wooden table with a gold "lucky cat" on it, the arm waving, supposedly bringing prosperity.

I collapsed on the sofa.

A little girl in a Teenage Mutant Ninja Turtles T-shirt walked out from behind a curtain.

"*Nǐ hǎo!*" I greeted.

"*Nǐ hǎo!*" she parroted back, holding a yellow stuffed tiger. She offered up her precious toy to me.

"*Shay shay.*"

I cradled the furry tiger in my arms and began to pet it.

A young mother with a messy bun and a small white towel over one shoulder ran into the reception area.

"Hello," she said, before speaking in Mandarin to her daughter. I wondered if she'd just scolded her. I couldn't tell.

She reached for her little girl's hand, then she took the tiger from my arms.

"Massage? Yes?" she asked.

"Yes." I held up two fingers.

"Ahhh, two hour."

I nodded and followed her behind the curtain and into a large room filled with more curtains.

Many of the curtains were closed—occupied with clients. We reached an empty cot, where she motioned for me to lie down while she drew the gold velvet drapes.

Shortly after, someone arrived and began working on my feet.

I drifted off to sleep, only to be woken by a nudge and told, "All done."

I looked at my watch and double-checked my per diem envelope.

There was just enough left for one more massage.

# 81

THE CAB DRIVER PULLED UP TO THE SIDEWALK AND BEGAN stacking my luggage. I stepped out and onto the curb just in time to see him lift my second suitcase from the trunk. It was bigger and heavier than he was.

I placed cash plus a tip into his sweaty palm. He nodded, smiling.

Once inside, I found China Eastern Air, queued up, and waited until my turn.

"*Nǐ hǎo.*" I handed my passport to the lady in a red dress with a blue logo embroidered on the right side of her mandarin collar. She looked at my ticket before she thumbed through each page of my passport.

I dragged my first suitcase, dropping it on the conveyer belt.

She looked over at the scale, pursed her lips while examining my photo, and then said something to me in Mandarin.

"I'm sorry, I don't speak Mandarin."

She studied my passport for a moment, then looked up from it to look down at me and said, "Too fat. Must pay."

My heart began to race, like I had too many cappuccinos. When I'd set aside travel money yesterday morning, I had forgotten to factor in excess baggage money. I'd squandered all my per diem on my day of decadence. I shouldn't have had that last massage. I shouldn't have had the last *two* massages. I reached for my per diem envelope and counted out what was left in front of her.

She motioned for me to put the second suitcase on the scale.

I inhaled, sucking my stomach in as if that would make the suitcase slimmer, and waited for the numbers to appear.

"Too fat, too," she insisted as she shook her head before she leaned over to the ticket agent next to her.

I counted my money again, hoping it had multiplied while I stood there.

It had not.

The agent leaned back into her seat and looked me in the eyes. "One hundred yuan."

I collected all the money on the counter and counted it out in front of her, again. "Twenty, thirty, forty, sixty, seventy, one, two, three, four." I looked up at her imploringly. She stood a good foot higher than me on a platform. I was a little girl again. Insecure. Powerless. Not understanding the words. "This is all I have."

"One hundred yuan," she demanded.

I showed her my empty envelope and followed that with my empty palms, like I did when I was out of dog treats with Ron Howard.

"I don't have any more." I shook my head.

She took the money from the counter and counted it again in Mandarin.

My palms began to sweat.

She counted it a second time.

I shifted my weight from one foot to the other while she leaned over and consulted with her colleague again.

I held my breath.

The agent began typing into her computer.

The sound of a printer.

"Okay," she grunted as she attached the tags to my bags for Kunming.

"*Shay shay*," I said with a smile, exhaling so hard I thought I was going to pass out.

# 82

OVERWHELMED WITH RELIEF, I STROLLED OVER TO THE LARGE screen displaying departure gates and found the word KUNMING. As I turned around to look for the gate, I did a double take.

*Cinderella? Impossible.*

But there she was, standing on a suitcase cart, on *top* of a suitcase, on *top* of her basket, watching all the comings and goings of the airport. Sunny stood at the head of the cart, reading a piece of paper.

"Sunny! *Wǒ gǎndào hěn kāixīn! Wǒ gǎndào hěn kāixīn!*" I shouted as I ran toward them.

"Cinderella and I are so happy to see you, too!" She giggled as I reached over and picked up Cinderella, who began licking my face as she wagged her tail.

"Why are you still here? I thought you left earlier yesterday morning!"

"They told me it would take three days before a plane leaves that will fly Cinderella."

"What?"

"Three days before a plane flying to Shanghai will take a dog," Sunny confirmed.

"That's awful! I'm so sorry. What will you do?"

"Don't worry." She reached over and stroked Cinderella's head. "I know someone who lives here in Lijiang and we'll stay until Cinderella can go home with me. She's coming to get me now."

A twentysomething hipster sidled up to Sunny. They embraced and I smiled.

"I'm so glad you have a friend here!"

"Me, too," she said. "We must go now."

"Send me photos."

I gave Cinderella a kiss and sat her back on her basket.

Sunny smiled and hugged me again before she pointed me in the direction of my departure gate.

The airport was small, basically an open hangar with only a few gates, so I didn't have far to go. I passed a gift shop filled with all the merchandise I'd seen in town and a tea and coffee shop that smelled so caffeinated it made my mouth water. But there would be no cappuccino this morning. I fantasized about all the ATMs I would hit in the Hong Kong airport that would buy me all the lattes I could drink, just two short plane rides away.

In my first airport café, I'd have a double cappuccino with almond milk frothed so thick I'd wear a white mustache while I sat back in my seat, talking to Mavis and Ron, letting them know I was on my way home. Then, that double would be followed by a single shot of espresso sipped next to an oversized window, watching jumbo jets take off and land while I dined on a warmed cinnamon roll fresh from the oven.

The last gate in the corner had a sign that read KUNMING. A dozen chairs sat scattered. One was unoccupied, so I claimed it. It happened to be the best seat to watch the comings and goings of the most happening place, where breakfast was now in full swing. Every seat was occupied at the U-shaped counter that surrounded the kitchen.

A short wait line stood just outside the eatery. At the head, a tall, thin man read a folded newspaper while he was talking on his mobile. I wondered, was he was reading something to the other person on the phone or was he was bored with the other person? Maybe he wasn't reading the paper at all.

Behind him, a young couple leaned against each other with neck rests around their necks, texting, never looking up from their screens.

Seated at the counter, a man dressed in a Western pin-striped business suit that he'd paired with plastic slip-on sandals and black socks slurped down his morning noodles.

Next to him sat an old woman in a navy, mandarin-collared tunic dress with matching trousers. I watched her devour a couple of hard-boiled eggs, masticating yellow and white food with dark, tobacco-stained teeth. Her tongue moved like a serpent trying to survive its demise while the young boy next to her scarfed down a bowl of congee.

My stomach grumbled and rumbled to the sounds of pots and pans clanging. The sizzling and searing from the grill blared like a loudspeaker over the mumbling of Mandarin, making me long for one last sticky bun. The smell of garlic pushed my salivary glands into overdrive. I swallowed hard, closed my eyes, and waited for boarding.

# 83

UPON ARRIVAL IN KUNMING, I DEPLANED AND MOVED alongside the other passengers huddled together like the mass migration of the wildebeest on the Serengeti. I followed signs that read CONNECTING FLIGHTS in tiny block letters beneath large Mandarin characters. I stood with my pack, watching them one by one collect their suitcases—typically something small, only one case, unassuming, sometimes just a plastic bag with duct tape wrapped around it—while I waited for my two overweight bags to arrive. I would be flying China Eastern Airlines again, this time to Hong Kong.

I handed over my passport and ticket to a guy in his twenties, wearing black-rimmed glasses and a neatly pressed white shirt with a red tie. He flipped through my passport like he was skimming a magazine while he motioned for me to lift my first bag onto the conveyer belt beside him.

"Your bag is overweight," he announced without looking up as the bag moved down the conveyor belt while he motioned for the other suitcase. "Fifty yuan."

My heart started to beat faster while my breathing became shallow, almost nonexistent as I watched him look at the number light up beside him.

"Another fifty yuan. One hundred yuan total," he said as he looked up at me.

"But I paid my overweight baggage in Lijiang. I thought that was supposed to get me to Hong Kong."

"One hundred yuan from Kunming to Hong Kong."

"I don't have any money to pay for more overweight baggage."

He stared at me for a brief moment, then looked back at my passport and my ticket.

"I spent all my money on overweight baggage in Lijiang," I pleaded.

He shook his head, jumped out of his chair, and walked over to the desk beside him, where an older woman sat with her hair pulled back tight in a bun. She wore Chinese-red lipstick, perfectly applied. They walked over together, stood tall on the platform behind the desk, and looked down at me.

I took a big breath in and let it out. The rest of her makeup was impeccable. The eyeliner perfectly drawn. Her eye shadow blended to perfection. In a red dress with a navy-blue scarf around her neck, she looked down at me with an expressionless face.

"We have overweight baggage fees. Extra charge one hundred yuan."

"I understand and I'm terribly sorry, but I don't have any money." I let out another breath before I began again. I repeated what I told the young man and added, "I thought that would pay for my bags to get all the way to Hong Kong."

"You have no money?"

"I have no money."

She took a good look at me—the one I was very familiar with by now, from my head to my toes and back up again.

I hung my head.

Shame overwhelmed me.

Shame for all the massages I had in Lijiang.

All the cappuccinos I drank in Shaxi.

For not preparing for emergencies like this.

For traveling with all these things in two monster-size bags when everyone traveled with so little here.

She bit her lip while her eyes looked past me.

"Okay, you can go," she said before she flipped the switch for my bags to go out to the plane, then shoved my ticket at me. "Take a seat until your flight is called."

*In March of 1971, the day after my ninth birthday, my mother moved to London.*

*Every week a postcard arrived—each front a different tableau . . .*

*Teddy bears at tea parties.*

*Hedgehogs dressed as bobbies.*

*Rabbits talking on the telly in bright red boxes.*

*These scenes provided insight into her new life. I saved each one and made a huge poster to hang on my bedroom wall so I could be with her.*

*We never spoke on the phone. It was too expensive.*

*It was the summer of 1973.*

*I was eleven.*

*My sister was three.*

*We went to see my mommy for the first time since she left Detroit that cold and dreary day.*

*Daddy flew with us on a 747 to New York's LaGuardia Airport.*

Then we got into a helicopter. It was noisy as the blades whipped through the air that bright sunny day while we crossed the city.

I could see tall buildings, bridges, and rivers.

Once we landed at JFK, Daddy took us to a gate that said LON-DON HEATHROW where he handed us over to the nice stewardess, Cindy. She wore a groovy powder-blue minidress with matching go-go boots and held our hands while a man in a three-piece suit said I wasn't old enough to travel internationally with someone under five.

And my sister wasn't old enough to travel without an adult.

Daddy yelled, "I didn't travel a plane and a helicopter to not get them on that plane!"

After a heated discussion, they made an exception.

Cindy walked us to the back of the plane so we could sit close to her while she ran the kitchen. She gave us coloring books and crayons, a deck of cards, and airplane wings that we pinned on our dresses. After she served dinner and cleaned up the kitchen, she took us to see the captain, where we got to watch him fly the plane in the dark.

When we landed, Mommy was waiting at the gate. She threw her arms around us and cried while she told us how big we had gotten.

She looked the same.

Tall, thin.

Long, straight red hair.

Really pretty, like always.

We collected our suitcases and got on the underground to Holland Park where we walked to the house that my mother shared with her two housemates, Pru and Izzy. Next door lived an old man with a spider monkey named Oscar.

She took us to the zoo, Henry VIII's palace, and to Fortnum & Mason for tea and scones. I liked teatime.

It rained a lot.

I cried a lot.

Daddy never let me cry.

If I did he said, "I'll give you something to cry about."

When I got home, Daddy had moved us to Newton, North Carolina, where I started the sixth grade a week late.

Two big girls wanted to beat me up after school because I was new and talked funny.

# 84

IN FRONT OF THE THREE CHECK-IN DESKS STOOD FOUR ROWS of chairs. The chairs sat empty with only a couple of people, so I took a seat, front and center, and began to collect myself. I closed my eyes and took a big breath in, and I let it out. I wanted to cry, I was so tired and hungry. I reached for a tissue in my pocket and pulled out Ron's tennis ball. I held it in my hand. I missed Max. He would have made this so much easier.

But I had made it! I got myself through a whole day on my own in Lijiang to Kunming with my bags on the plane to Hong Kong. All I had to do now was wait for my flight to be called and board.

Most of my flight looked like businessmen. I did not spot another non-Asian. Everyone's transactions seemed smooth, uncomplicated. One small bag checked. Occasionally a passenger would take a seat where I sat but most walked through a guarded walkway.

A woman dressed in a military uniform walked out from the office area. "Lisa Cheek."

"Yes." I jumped up, threw my backpack over my shoulder, grabbed my carry-on, ready to take my seat on the plane, and followed her through a secured door, down a long hallway, past two small, occupied offices, until we entered a small office with no windows. There was a desk with a chair at one end of the room, with a well-worn brown sofa at the other. We stood in between the two. Fluorescent lights flickered and hummed from the ceiling.

"We have canceled your flight."

"Canceled my flight? What do you mean you canceled my flight?" I asked as I began to feel faint from hunger.

"We canceled your flight," she reiterated.

"I watched my bags leave on the conveyer belt."

"We took your bags off the plane."

"You mean the plane is not leaving?"

"The plane is leaving. You are not."

"What?" I reached for the edge of the sofa and sat down. "I don't understand."

She towered over me, watching me as I tried to piece together what she had just told me. "But I have my ticket." I held it up to show it to her.

A skinny male officer with a blue jacket and short brimmed hat entered the tiny room and handed my passport to the woman, who turned to me and said, "Miss Cheek, your visa expired."

"What? No!"

"You overstayed your visa."

"No. That's not possible."

"You stayed too long."

"My visa is good for six months," I informed her. She clearly didn't understand.

"Your visa is good for thirty days within those six months listed on the visa," she corrected me.

"No! That's not what they told me!" I shook my head. "My

visa is good for six months. That's what the man told me. He told me it was good for six months."

"You must pay five thousand yuan."

"Five thousand yuan?" I shook my head, not believing what she was saying. My lower lip started to quiver. Snot filled my ear canals and sinuses. Tears welled up. Thoughts of a dingy, dirty, dark prison with no food and screams of madness in Mandarin flooded my mind. "Five thousand yuan? But I don't have any money."

"I take you to ATM."

"But my ATM card doesn't work here on the mainland." I sniveled. "It's only for Bank of China accounts."

"You try."

# 85

WE DESCENDED AN OPEN, CIRCULAR STAIRCASE THAT OVERLOOKED the entire Kunming airport. People were busy, buying tickets, checking bags. As we walked farther down, people stopped and stared. I felt like Norma Desmond getting ready for my close-up, but once we hit the ground floor and began across the vast main room, the stops and stares and whispers felt more like *Dead Man Walking*—life as I'd known it was about to end. The loud departure activity had become silent, like a library. I was guided from one side of the amphitheater-size room to the other, bumping into passengers with airplane tickets, tripping over their bags as they stopped to watch me be escorted. Now they not only had a plane ticket but a matinee ticket to my Chinese drama and were about to witness my fate as we approached the ATM.

We stopped and stared at the large white wall where my freedom was encased and approached the machine together as if it were some great guru gifting me the keys to the kingdom . . . or just my ticket out of here.

I studied the signage outside of the machine, looking for the Cirrus and Pulse logos, known for their worldwide representation on ATMs that allowed users to withdraw money all over the world.

Neither were visible here.

Only one very large logo.

*The Bank of China.*

I looked back at the official, hoping for a reprieve, wanting to explain to her that I wouldn't get any money here, that this machine would not like my card.

I closed my eyes and prayed, "God, please give me five thousand yuan so I may go home." Then I inserted my card and began to enter my pin numbers. The machine spat the card back out.

"Try again," she said.

I inserted the card in the slot and it was spat back out.

I squeezed my eyes closed to hold back the tears.

"No money. You cannot leave China." She tightened her grip around my tricep and moved us back through the crowd like a plane navigating through a storm—quickly and with ease, only allowing me to stumble over someone's bag once on our way back to the office, where I took my seat on the ratty old couch to cry while I rummaged through my backpack to find some tissues and Ron's tennis ball.

The male official entered the room with my passport in hand and chatted to my kidnapper, catching up on our latest escapades, occasionally looking my way. I'd catch a glance while reaching for more tissues. It was as if they were trying to size me up. Finally my hostage taker asked, "Can you call someone to bring money?"

"I can try," I sniveled.

I blew my nose one more time, wiped my tears, and reached for my phone. Max had made a list of phone numbers for me in case of emergency, so I started at the top and dialed Robert's number. It rang.

I looked up at my ransom holders.

They both looked back at me with folded arms.

On the final ring, it connected to Robert's voicemail.

"Robert, it's Lisa. I'm being detained at the Kunming airport for overstaying my visa. They want five thousand yuan. Please call me back." My toe kicked at the chipped vinyl flooring. "I'm being held in a little room with no windows. Thanks. Bye."

I looked up at my captors. "Do I get another phone call 'cause he didn't answer?"

One of them nodded.

I looked at my list. Everyone was traveling today. I left Eva and Max voicemails before I looked back up at my abductors. "May I go to the restroom?"

"I'll take you."

With a firm grip, I was escorted down another small, dark hallway, which ended and turned right. On the left was a door.

"I wait for you here," she informed me as she stood just outside.

As soon as the door closed behind me, I leaned over to brace myself and cried. I had called all the numbers I had and no one picked up. I was left alone to rot in a prison in Kunming. I would never see Ron Howard again. All for five thousand yuan.

I cried until there was nothing left. Then I blew my nose and fumbled around my backpack, discarding all the used tissues in the trash container. I took a breath and leaned over the sink. I threw water on my face and washed my hands before I opened the door to rejoin my capturer. She took ahold of my arm and escorted me back to the tiny office, where I took "my seat" on the sofa.

My stomach growled. I was famished, so I rummaged around

my carry-on, unable to find anything edible. I pulled out the only book I'd brought, *One Hundred Years of Solitude*, and looked at the cover. My destiny.

# 86

THE MALE OFFICIAL STOPPED IN AGAIN. THEY EXCHANGED A FEW words, never taking their eyes off of me. I looked down at my tennis shoe. The big toe on the right foot had a hole in the top. It must be from all the uneven streets I'd walked the past three months. The end of the shoelace on the left foot was frayed and filthy from the dirty walkways and streets. I thought about Ron and wondered if he knew I was stranded trying to get back to him. How badly I wanted to get home, where my friends and family were. There truly was no place like home, and I wanted to be there now. My phone rang.

"Hello?"

"Lisa, Robert here!"

"ROBERT!"

"So you need some money."

"I do. I'm sorry. I was told my visa was good for six months."

"Don't worry. We are working on it."

"Five thousand yen?"

"We have someone who lives in Kunming. They will bring you the money. It may take a few hours, but we'll get you on a flight. So sit tight."

"Thank you."

"They're going to bring the money soon."

I let my captors know the bail money was on its way.

# 87

"A MAN TO SEE YOU," ONE OF MY ABDUCTORS ANNOUNCED.

There, standing before me, dressed in blue jeans, a red T-shirt, and his "Little Sister" baseball cap with an envelope in one hand and Mei Mei in the other, stood Vin.

"*Nǐ hǎo!!!*" I screamed as I leaped off the sofa to give him a hug. "*Wǒ gǎndào hěn kāixīn. Wǒ gǎndào hěn kāixīn!!!*"

Vin handed the envelope to the officer and Mei Mei to me.

"*Shay shay*, Vin! *Shay shay*!" I blubbered while tears rained down on Mei Mei's head. I looked at the tall, lanky man who had greeted me at this very airport three months ago, chain-smoking.

My hero.

The man who lugged my suitcases up and down stairs and drove along uneven roads like he was a competitor for Mr. Universe.

The man who provided little Mei Mei a forever home.

The man who would see to it that I would go home.

The uniformed official returned to the room and handed me my passport.

"Last plane to Hong Kong leaves in fifteen minutes. Your bags are on board."

I turned to look at Vin. "I must go now. *Wǒ gǎndào hěn kāixīn!*"

I kissed Mei Mei's head, handed her back to Vin, and then grabbed him around the neck for a quick hug.

Vin nodded.

"Time to go or you will miss your flight," the official reiterated.

I reached for my backpack and looked back at Vin and Mei Mei one last time, smiled, and then felt a hand guide my elbow down the dimly lit hallway through another door and out to the departure area—up the jetway to my seat on the plane.

I fastened my seat belt, and as I waited for takeoff, I thought about all the people who had loved and cared for me, who didn't speak a word of English, yet there was so much deep communication—heartfelt communication. Kindness is the universal language and can be spoken anywhere without uttering a word. It's the magic in our lives.

True fairy tales are when we save ourselves through the things we learn. My life had been forever changed knowing that, no matter where I went, there would always be people who wanted to help, nurture, and love me. I just needed to let them.

*Shay shay.*

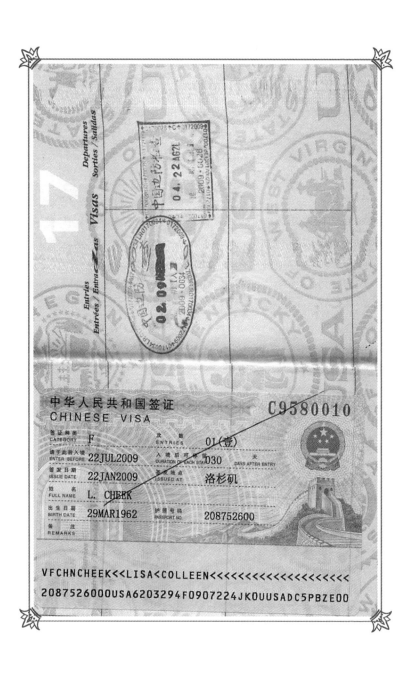

Departures
Sorties / Salidas

17

Entries
Entrées / Entradas

Visas

中华人民共和国签证
CHINESE VISA

C9580010

签证种类
CATEGORY          F

次数
ENTRIES          01(壹)

请于此者入境
ENTER BEFORE     22JUL2009

入境后可停留
DURATION OF EACH STAY  030

天
DAYS AFTER ENTRY

签发日期
ISSUE DATE       22JAN2009

签发地点
ISSUED AT        洛杉矶

姓名
FULL NAME        L. CHEEK

出生日期
BIRTH DATE       29MAR1962

护照号码
PASSPORT NO.     208752600

备注
REMARKS

VFCHNCHEEK<<LISA<COLLEEN<<<<<<<<<<<<<<<<<<<<
2087526000USA6203294F0907224JKOUUSADC5PBZE00

# AUTHOR'S NOTE

Two months later, on June 25, 2009, after a twelve-hour day of editing our movie, I turned on the television and learned of Michael Jackson's death.

Most of what you read is true.

I changed names, created composites, and did my best with memories, photos, Facebook, and the web.

And I added a little fairy-tale magic.

# ACKNOWLEDGMENTS

To say I am grateful to the following people feels like an understatement, but none of this would have been put to the page had it not been for their generosity, love, and encouragement.

So, *shay shay* to . . .

My very own Fairy Godmother, Amy Ferris, who makes dreams come true. She showed me how to write, edit, and publish a book. I am the luckiest girl to know and love her.

Andrea Frazer Paventi, who took me to coffee and said, "You need a mentor." Not only did she hook me up with Amy but she added the final magic touches to my book. (Plus she's the best friend a girl could have.)

Max Chan, my assistant on the film, who made my experience on the mainland and Hong Kong unforgettable. I couldn't imagine editing this movie without him.

Richard Bowen and the film crew, especially the camera crew, who were the best housemates ever!

Debra Landwehr Engle, my spiritual teacher, who taught me it's all about love.

Nancy Sarnoff for creating Perfect Pet and for rescuing Ron Howard. Without that adventurous dog, there would be no story to tell.

David Paul Kirkpatrick, who gave me a writers' community where I belonged.

Jack Grapes, who not only taught me how to write an image moment but throws the best parties in all of Hollywood in each and every class.

Roni Keller, whose encouragement is why any of my stories have ever hit a page. Thank you for going to class with me every Thursday.

My twin sister, Jill Sherer-Murray. I'm older, but she's prettier and funnier. Thank you for your love and patience.

My Thursday writers group: Debbie C, Debbie K and Aysu. My Sunday writers group: Dragan, Kathryn, Lisa, and Elden. My Wednesday writers' group: Susan, Lisa, Cindy, Sylvia, and Merry.

Brooke Warner, for saying, "We'd be honored to publish it."

Everyone at She Writes Press.

Dad and Mom, for showing me the magic of books.

Betty, who showed me how joyful writing can be.

Alvin and Josephine Simone, my adorable mutts, who have taught me how to be in the moment.

Ron Howard, a.k.a. Theodore, The Adorable, The Adored, Theo—a soul unlike any other who loved me when I couldn't love myself and taught me how to love unconditionally.

Adopt a mutt—they are life-changing.

And my very own Prince Charming, Christopher Dain Maxwell Johnson, "Big Johnson," who has loved and adored me and believed in me. You are the best husband today and every day! Thank you for teaching me how to dream big! How to love big! How to be BIG!

## ABOUT THE AUTHOR

photo credit to Carina Hildebrandt

After twenty-five years editing and producing other people's work, Lisa decided to take her coworkers' advice and tell her own stories. She currently lives in Los Angeles with her two mutts, Alvin and Josephine Simone; her two cats, Trixie and Eartha Kitt; and her husband, Chris Johnson. Most days you can find her dancing to Motown or Madonna and working on her next book.

Wanna connect?
Author Website: lisacheek.com
Substack: lisacheek.substack.com
Instagram: @lisacheekauthor
Facebook: lisacheekauthor

## Looking for your next great read?

We can help!

Visit www.shewritespress.com/next-read
or scan the QR code below for a list
of our recommended titles.

She Writes Press is an award-winning
independent publishing company founded to
serve women writers everywhere.